Meditation and Mindfulness for Beginners

Let go, Find Peace and Enjoy Every Moment

Natalie Morgon

Table of Contents

Introduction

The moment you are experiencing right now will never happen again. You will never be this age, on this day, in this place precisely the same way. Life changes in small and significant ways all the time, usually without your consent. Your life is a river, moving and flowing and always going forward.

How do we enjoy every moment? Is it possible to savor it, like a delicious meal with a loved one? Pictures and videos may help us snatch a moment from time, framing it for us to enjoy forever, but that moment will soon be the past.

This book will help you live in the present moment, focus on every moment, and soak it up for all its worth. Even the hard moments and seasons of life are valuable and deserve to be honored for what they are and what they can teach us. We live in a fast-paced world that focuses on the future, so it can be incredibly challenging to slow down and embrace every day, every hour, and every breath we take.

It's not impossible. Mindfulness is available to everyone, no matter what age or life circumstance. You don't have to feel ashamed of your desire to slow down and take control of your mental health. In fact, you should applaud yourself for putting something so important in the forefront of your mind.

Your journey begins here.

Chapter 1: Mindfulness

What mindfulness is and what it is not

Mindfulness is not something you do and check off your list; it is a way of life. It's a choice to be aware, to be present, and to show up as yourself without hiding or judging. It's also not tied to any one religion or spirituality but adopted by people of all faiths and beliefs to ground themselves, heal from trauma, and achieve personal growth.

Mindfulness is being aware and present on purpose. Not to be confused with meditation, which is a practice that clears the mind. Mindfulness is different because you are aware of thoughts and present to them without clearing them and letting them go completely.

It can be a tricky intertwining of ideas, but both mindfulness and meditation, while different, are based on the same premise. They both promote self-awareness and help you connect with your deepest, innermost being.

Benefits of mindfulness

Anytime we take a moment to slow everything down, it will help significantly to reduce stress. It will also regulate physiological functions like heart rate and blood pressure. Your attention, focus and brain function may increase as well.

Those who struggle with anxiety and depression may approach mindfulness to regulate their emotions in order to improve their quality of life. Most people who suffer from mental illnesses feel trapped and controlled. Learning to use mindfulness as a tool can help release some of that pressure, allowing a person to feel more emotionally stable.

We all have our coping mechanisms that we use to deal with the stressors of life. Some people enjoy eating and then turn toward overeating, binging, or stress eating in times of trouble. Others dive into self-absorbed activities that push them away from their feelings and other people.

They are scared or ashamed of their feelings and therefore choose to ignore their problems. Others choose destructive behaviors until they finally hit rock bottom and realize they need help.

Mindfulness is a type of healthy coping mechanism. It is a tool in your toolkit to help manage emotions instead of pushing them away. This lifestyle is something you can use anywhere and anytime. You aren't dependent on an exercise gym or exercise mat.

The key benefit is that it gets to the root of the issue. Mindfulness isn't a band-aid, but a scalpel. Though it sounds painful and will be sometimes, the benefits of digging deep far outweigh the harm we do to ourselves if we continue to ignore our pain points and stressors.

Mindful moment

Many benefits come from taking short mindful breaks throughout the day. Short mindful breaks will loosen you up physically and emotionally, giving you the strength and courage to move on with whatever you are facing that day.

Small, mindful moments can be as easy as closing your eyes for one minute and focusing on your breathing. Breathe in through your nose and out through your mouth. You can count your breaths, or simply listen and feel the air fill your lungs and then release.

Another easy mindfulness strategy is to take a brisk walk. This can even be up and down a set of stairs if you are working and can't get away. Getting outside for five minutes to say hello to the sun and feel the fresh air across your cheeks works wonders. It reminds you that you are not alone, and the world is big and beautiful, much bigger, and more beautiful than your problems.

I know you can't control the weather, but one mindful moment that everyone can have is to observe and pay attention to a simple experience of rain. Rain is typically a nuisance when you have made plans outside, have done your hair a certain way, or need to drive somewhere. Rainstorms can be scary and even dangerous.

But what if you stopped and experienced the rainfall for the first time? Pay attention to the sounds, the smells, and the sight of it. Allow yourself to be wrapped up in the beauty of the phenomenon we take for granted all the time. Think about all the good the rain is doing for the earth, and for yourself. Pause what you are doing and get closer to the rain to truly experience it without barriers.

In this mindful moment, you are tuning in to your senses and letting yourself slow down to appreciate an act of nature. Rain has a certain smell as it drops into the ground where the water mixes with the dirt.

The sound of rain can take on many forms depending on how fast the wind is blowing or where the rain hits when it falls. Raindrops on the pavement sound different from a tin roof or tree leaves.

Close your eyes and if you are brave, walk around in it. Feel the drop in temperature around you or the chill of raindrops hitting your skin. After you have an immersive experience with a common rainfall, you might be surprised about how grounded you feel afterward.

Human being vs human doing

Imagine a room full of kids all dressed in colorful clothes. They are wearing headbands, hats, and socks with little bells that jingle when they walk. Their joy is evident on their faces.

On the other hand, they are also chewing gum loudly, talking expressively with their friends and fidgeting their hands around constantly.

This is our life; Constant movement, and noises everywhere. Every time you turn around there are more people who don't stop doing or moving and never seem to rest.

One of the best things you can do for yourself is to give up the notion that you can do it all or have it all. You are a human being, and life is a gift. You are not what you do, and you are not what you accomplish.

If we walk into a room and someone asks us to introduce ourselves, we will always talk about what we do. But what if we talked about who we are? What we love? What our character is like, and what makes us feel loved and at ease?

We are who we are on purpose, and nothing we do or don't do will take away our intrinsic value. It's important for us to speak truth and love to our minds and our bodies. We accomplish that through mindfulness.

Nothing is more important than loving yourself and having the confidence to face whatever comes your way. Inner strength keeps our heads held high when everything around us is falling apart. You owe it to yourself to notice your best qualities and appreciate who you are, not what you do.

Doing that comes out of being

But of course, we have to "do." We have to work, take care of people, figure out what's for dinner and stop at the grocery to buy what we need to achieve that. But in our doing, can we be peaceful? Can we live out every moment with peace and contentment?

Being mindful throughout the day is difficult. Exactly one million things distract us and staying focused is an Olympic feat. Mindful moments will help bring us back to focus when we are losing it, and that's why it is important to take brief breaks.

Mindful moments are needed every once in a while, to reset and recharge. But throughout the day, we can pay attention to what's happening around us and in us.

When someone at work says something, and we feel a ping in our hearts, we can stop and think about that ping. What does it mean? What emotion can I name it? Why does it hurt, and what can I do about it? If not, then jot yourself a note and think about it on the way home when you can leave the radio off, breathe deeply, and be mindful of your emotions.

Mindfulness isn't always solving things in the moment or knowing what they are. But it is the act of paying attention, which means you don't have the luxury of ignoring or stuffing feelings that come up.

Non-judging is an act of intelligence and kindness

If you are not in the habit of noticing how much judgment comes into play as you have thoughts and experience feelings, this information may come as a surprise. Every thought and emotion we have triggers a judgment.

We label things as "good" or "bad" pretty quickly. As soon as we label or judge something, more emotions and thoughts are triggered based on that judgment. Things can get out of control if we don't stop and sit with that first emotion instead of following the downward spiral.

As we learn not to judge what comes to our mind as black or white, good or bad, up or down, etc; we can then use discernment to weigh the emotion or thought. This will lead to better decisions and more thought-out choices that affect us and those around us.

Non-judging is an act of kindness because it allows for compassion and love. Non-judging gives us the tools to say the things to ourselves that we would say to a beloved friend.

When we make a mistake, non-judging helps us to evaluate the situation without throwing ourselves so far under the bus in shame and regret that it's difficult to drag ourselves back up. To have the courage to move forward and do better next time, we must be gentle and kind to ourselves.

Known mindfulness facts

Fact #1: Mindfulness changes our brains for the better: Studies have shown that mindfulness can increase the gray matter used in our memory, focus, attention span, and even creativity.

Fact #2: Mindfulness can help develop empathy: Because mindfulness helps decrease the time in which we react to emotions, people who practice mindfulness are better prepared to deal with another person's emotions without judgment or harsh reactions.

Mindfulness also helps with decision-making and clear thinking so we can see another's point of view and experiences more clearly.

Fact #3: Mindfulness can promote a positive body image: People who practice mindfulness and positive self-talk enjoy more positive body awareness and experience.

Because our society focuses heavily on appearance and perfectionism, some people are tortured by it. Mindfulness can help turn around the narrative and allow everyone to appreciate their bodies in a new way.

Myths of mindfulness

Myth #1: Mindfulness is part of a religion: Most people think that only those who follow the religion of Buddhism practice mindfulness. While many Buddhists use mindfulness as part of expressing their religion, anyone with any religion can practice mindfulness.

Because it is a way of life, it does not adhere to doctrine, theology, or pragmatic rules. It is a way of life that anyone who wants to try it can adopt.

Myth #2: Mindfulness is hard: While learning something new poses a challenge, developing a mindfulness practice is possible. You can start with as little as one minute each day, just focusing on your breath. This may not seem like a lot, but a little goes a long way. If the "professionals" intimidate you, then take a minute to list out all the reasons you are feeling fearful or inadequate.

Use this time to enter yourself into the "beginner" category and let yourself off the hook. Even if it is hard for you at first, with time, you will find your rhythm.

Myth #3: You have to be mindful the whole day: While mindfulness is something you can use throughout your day as a tool, it is not realistic to be mindful every second of every day. Instead, think of mindfulness as a checkpoint.

When you are feeling stressed or need to check in with your mind and body, take a minute to do so and practice mindfulness using the foundations you will learn below. Don't be too hard on yourself and expect perfection but take advantage of the mindset to help you pay attention to what's going on.

Myth #4: The goal of mindfulness is to be relaxed all the time: While it is helpful to practice mindfulness and meditation to relax and be less stressed, that is not the only purpose. As you pursue mindfulness, you will be asked to be present with your thoughts, feelings, and experiences. This may feel uncomfortable and require you to deal with suppressed pain.

Attitudinal foundations of mindfulness practice

Taking a step toward mindful living is brave and to be admired. It is challenging to choose a way of life that opens you up more fully to yourself and the world. This can be terrifying in a way. But as with any new adventure, we need to have our gear.

A hiker setting out to climb a mountain will have proper hiking boots, thick socks, a walking pole, weather-appropriate clothes, and a light backpack. Just like a hiker, we can be prepared too.

Here are seven attitudinal foundations to help you establish a mindfulness practice. Keep in mind that you may be learning about some of these for the first time, so have grace and patience with yourself as you navigate this unfamiliar territory.

Non-judging

We are so attached to judging that we don't even realize that we are doing it. Our minds categorize every experience as either positive, negative, or indifferent. This is an automatic response that we need to explore. Sometimes those judgments help us, but not every time. The constant judging can become overwhelming and unnecessary.

Going into mindfulness with an awareness of how much we judge our thoughts, feelings, and actions will help us recognize and consider the time and effort we put forth into judging. It can be surprising. The idea is not to stop judging all the time but to hold our judgments carefully in our hands like a porcelain doll and look at them. Consider. Question. Be curious. And then slowly release if need to be.

Our behaviors are connected to our thoughts, feelings, and values. In childhood, behaviors are praised or criticized, so something conditioned us to react to the way we were treated over time, and as our brains develop, we can think and act for ourselves. Many adults spend hours in therapy untangling the strings of messages they have heard their whole life and are understanding just now.

Non-judging is important because some things you feel or believe about yourself may actually be someone else's projection on you. It's crucial to consider what rises in us and where the source is. When you are practicing mindfulness, and you feel a strong emotion rise, stop the reaction. Consider, question, and be curious about that emotion and your natural subsequent reaction. Be quiet in your innermost self and recognize the judgment that you place on the emotion, the response, and yourself.

With time, you will seek out alternative ways to process through and cope with your emotions, thoughts, and judgments. It is crucial to practice non-judging in your mindfulness practices, as it will unlock deeper truths for yourself.

Patience

It's no secret that humans have more difficulty with patience in this fast-paced world. We nurse our ego so much that waiting for almost anything feels unjust. We don't like to admit how impatient we are, but it is the truth.

We like the idea of patience, and we all want more. But we struggle through the necessary steps to become a more patient person. Mindfulness is an excruciatingly patient way of life. Your selfish tendencies will yell at the top of their lungs for you to move on, but mindful practice will teach you to stay in it and keep breathing.

Patience isn't just waiting for something; it's retraining your body and mind not to be immediately satisfied. Progress does not come in a pill. In order to be a more patient, kind, gentle, and easy-going person, the work is daily and can feel daunting.

The best way to practice patience is to slow down. Think about going on a walk with a small child. They are fascinated by the most minute details, and you will roll your eyes when they bring you yet another rock but aren't they the happiest?

Doesn't that fifth rock thrill them to no end? We don't have to be happy with rocks, but we can practice noticing the little things. A small child has no cares in the world, no bills to pay, or cars to drive to appointments.

Children use their tiny fingers to discover and stay curious. Walking alongside them at their pace will do wonders for our personal growth. How can you slowdown in your life right now? How can you "stop and smell the roses?"

Beginner's mind

When you start your mindfulness journey, having a beginner's mind is crucial. You must clear your head of preconceptions and ideas. You may be thinking about another person's journey and the way they approach their mindful way of life.

While it's helpful to understand how others embrace mindfulness, you will approach it in your way. Everyone has a unique style and personality that brings mindfulness to life in a beautiful way.

Let's take the pressure off. Having a beginner's mind means you are open to what mindfulness will mean to you. You are willing to try new things without fear. Although you may be nervous about choosing what works for you and what doesn't, it's important to trust that you will get there in time. Trial and error are the name of the game, and that's nothing to be ashamed about.

Beginners are excited and have so much to learn. But they are also incredible listeners who are not jaded by experience. As you walk into this journey, keep an open mind, and pay attention to what mindfulness is opening up for you. What gets you excited? What new things do you want to try?

When someone mentions "mindful driving" or "mindful eating," and you don't know exactly what that means, enjoy the jolt of curiosity and excitement that flows through you.

Pick up books and magazines and read online articles that will help you gather more information. You have already made a great choice in reading this book to help open your world to all the possibilities. If you feel overwhelmed by all the options, then sit down and make a list of where you feel most energetic to begin. Start there, and with time, you will be helping others along in their mindfulness journey.

Gratitude is a great place to start while beginning the journey. You may not feel capable of even explaining what mindfulness means to you while you are just in the beginning stages. But try to be grateful for the little tidbits that you are learning.

The more you learn, the clearer things will be to you. You will pick and choose your favorite techniques and best practices that will benefit you in your current season of life. Have faith, everyone starts as a beginner first.

Trust

An entrepreneur CEO of a company will always be more invested in the company than the employees. Self-employed business owners who began with nothing and built an empire will tell you how much blood, sweat, and countless tears were involved. No one knows the company and business like the person who created it.

No one cares about it as much either. Only the owner who has been there since the beginning is as invested emotionally, financially, and mentally.

It is the same with you. You are the only you in the world. There is no other you. No one knows your mind, heart, soul, and body better than you. Every pressure point, every memory and painful photo from your past sparks something in you that others cannot feel.

It may feel like you dont blend in with the world, or don't have anything to offer. You are wrong; the world needs you to show up as your true self because no one else can take your place.

Now think about this; do you trust yourself? Do you trust your gut instincts and feelings as they wash over you? Or do you second guess everything, thinking that maybe you are mistaken and there's no hope for you to figure things out on your own?

Mindfulness requires you to open up and trust yourself in a deeper way than you have before. Your body is trying to tell you things, and it needs you to listen. It needs you to know that there are more profound things going on than you might realize at face value. With time, you will discern and tackle one thing at a time as you trust yourself through the process.

As you sit with yourself and go about your day, pay attention to how often you throw yourself under the bus or question your own decisions. Think about the basis of those accusations. Are you having second thoughts because someone else does things differently? Or you might be ashamed of who you are? If appropriate, go with what you feel strongly about, and don't look back.

Non-striving

We have goals and measures of success that we are constantly checking in with throughout our lives. It's easy to strive and push for that next level, the great promotion, the perfect body, or even a more peaceful mindset. We want to change things, progress, move forward and put the past behind us.

That kind of rushed living is not healthy. It goes back to the fact that you are a human being, not a human doing. It's essential to set aside your striving if you want to make genuine progress. Don't be fooled by a to-do list with boxes checked off.

Think about what striving has done to you. Reflect on your years and consider how striving in your personal or professional life might have damaged you. Maybe your physical health has been affected. Or, maybe your emotional health has taken a hit.

Without judging yourself or your past choices, examine the reasons behind your striving. Are you trying to prove something? What are you trying to prove, and to whom? Others? Yourself? Letting go of striving is not giving up on your goals.

It's simply shifting your goals to include your health; physical, mental, and emotional. If striving has not served you in the past, think about how you can live mindfully in a way that allows you to reach your goals without sacrificing something precious.

Imagine yourself at work or at a place where you have always pushed yourself to the limits. Maybe it's the gym where your self-hatred comes up and talks to you negatively, beating you up as you try to finish a workout. You end the workout feeling more defeated than energized because of the voices in your head.

Let's approach the gym with a non-striving mindset. Think about your goals as you walk into the gym, through the doors, and to your favorite corner. You set your things down and take one last sip of water. You breathe and think about what you want to accomplish this time. How is it different from last time? Your literal goal may still be the same: walk or run on the treadmill for 30 minutes.

But what if instead of beating yourself up for getting tired quickly, you set up regular intervals to walk? And while you are walking, you repeat mantras and encourage yourself. You thank your body for its hard work and the gift it is to you. If you have negative thoughts, you acknowledge them without judging and rewrite the narrative in a kind and gentle way.

Acceptance

Acceptance can be confused with approval, and therefore this concept can be difficult to understand at first. We want things to improve and be better, so why would we "accept" the way we are? Wouldn't that admit defeat?

You can still have goals and ideas of how to grow personally, but mindfulness calls you to humble yourself, and accept where you are right now. When you are paying attention to your mind and body, things may come up that you struggle to embrace as real. You may talk it away, wish it away, or blame someone or something else. However, the healthy step is to see yourself for who you are at the moment and be kind anyway.

Acceptance helps you make true change. It's not healthy to ignore a heart problem. Your first step is to get medical help and make a plan to move forward. It's the same thing with our emotional and mental health. When our bodies deliver news, we have to pay attention and accept what our bodies are telling us. It's the first plan of action.

It's hard to ask for help, and it's hard to admit when we are wrong. Acceptance is like raising your hand in a classroom when the teacher asks who needs after-school tutoring. It might humiliate you to admit that you have to stay after school and redo the problems on the worksheet that the entire class already turned in. But to get a good grade, you have to be honest with yourself. If you try too hard to keep up appearances, you might end up cheating or lying to your parents.

When you admit and accept that you need help, you believe the best about yourself. Because you know that with hard work, effort, and courage, you can do better.

Letting go

We have come to the end of the seven attitudinal foundations of mindfulness, and this is the last one. Non-judging helps you practice letting go of judgments for every single thought and feeling. It allows you to release the pressure to place things into categories.

Patience is required to let go of the rush momentum we experience in a fast-paced world. As we approach things with the eyes of a child who is curious and not in a hurry to get somewhere, we let go of goals and desires that don't mean much to us.

Having a beginner's mind is a brilliant way of letting go of the heightened desire to be an expert. We can be free to try new things without needing to be at the top of the class.

Establishing a healthy trust with ourselves encourages us to let go of the fear and lies that say we aren't good enough. We shed what has dragged us down for so long and instead cling to the gut instincts and beauty we can find in ourselves. As we adopt a mindset of non-striving, we let go of our place in the rat race of life. Non-striving is a gift to us that we can't have unless we let go of to-do lists that aren't getting us anywhere.

Acceptance is a beautiful way to let go of the masks we wear to hide who we really are. Acceptance opens up a new world of discovery; one which we previously ran away from because we didn't honestly acknowledge where we stood. Believing the truth about ourselves and swallowing our pride helps us let go of the past and move forward into the future with honesty.

Letting go is tough. We want to hold tight to so many things; things that are comfortable and familiar to us, like a worn couch or a pair of jeans we have had for years. It feels unnatural to release some things we have done for so long. True growth comes out of peeling away unwanted layers. It's painful but necessary.

Chapter 2: Beginner's mind

Who am I? Questioning our own narrative

It sounds loopy to talk about the voices in your head, but we all have them. We can trace phrases back to our childhood or even as recently as the last few years. There are certain things that we tell ourselves over and over, and that becomes our inner narrative or our "story."

Brené Brown tells us to notice the stories we are telling ourselves in her book, Rising Strong. She encourages us to speak the truth about the story we believe and to share that truth with those we love.

"The story I am telling myself" opens us up to admit what we believe in the moment, and it usually is the worst-case scenario. The story is not usually building us up but tearing us down. The story may be acting out of shame and guilt or believing someone else is thinking the worst of us.

So, ask yourself, who am I? What are the stories I am telling myself and believing? When you feel most vulnerable, what thoughts are digging deep tracks in your mind? What song is on repeat?

Pay attention to these. We will dig into what we can do with them. It's okay and even encouraged to question the narrative that defines our life. When you were in school, maybe you were the pretty one, or the smart one or the easy-going one.

Maybe people depended on you, and you felt you could never let them down, so you just went with the flow instead of asserting yourself. Narratives can change with time, and maybe you have found yourself in a new story after years of being someone else.

A new job or relationship or phase of life could send you spiraling into alternative stories that are equally harmful.

It's important to be mindful of the things that are on repeat. Our brains get stuck in cycles, and it's hard to break out of them. Your inner narrative will explain things the way it has always interpreted them, according to your story.

For example, let's say you are getting ready for work, and you can't find the right outfit to wear for your big presentation. You choose one outfit, but the colors seem too bold, and you think about how you used to get made fun of at school for wearing brightly colored and slightly obnoxious clothes.

Every outfit you pick up makes you feel insecure because it feels like "too much," and then you hear yourself repeating frantically in your mind, "You are just too much."

It's hard to regain confidence and choose an appropriate outfit when wheels from your past are spinning so hard you can't hear anything else.

You are more than any narrative

So, what do we do?

First, we calculate the accuracy of the inner narrator, the story, and the tracks laid. Is it true? Where did it come from? Does it help me at all? Most of the time, the inner narrator is not helpful. You can rise above past circumstances, past wounds, and past lies that you have believed for way too long.

You are more than any narrative. You are a unique and beautiful person who has more to offer this world than what you are giving yourself credit for. Mindfulness requires you to do some work, however. You must reset the tracks.

Celebrate the good and beautiful things about the struggles you are currently having. Referring back to the closet situation as you prepare for work, think about how we can rewrite that narrative. Instead of thinking of yourself as "too much," how can we reframe that?

We can acknowledge that growing up; our fashion choices were loud, creative, and colorful. Others did not always appreciate it, but you were trying your best and having fun.

So, let's take that fun into your closet and celebrate your creativity with an outfit that has a pop of color but tasteful pieces to maintain a professional image. Let's say you choose black pants, a neutral top, but a scarf with soft tones of springtime color to match your vibrant personality.

As you step out to work, you are refusing to believe the lie that you are "too much." You are believing the best about yourself and rising above the narrative. It's vital to your positive outlook to embrace your creativity and show it in doses that bring you joy and make you feel most like yourself.

With time, you can change your narrative as well. If you used to be fashionable and maybe a little over the top, maybe you can explore that in other areas of your life. Try a hobby that allows you to tap into that wild, colorful side. Art, music, hobbies, and literature can accentuate who you are and help you to not get embarrassed about it but embrace it!

You are whole

One of the beautiful things about mindfulness is that it brings you to a realization that you are a whole person with value and infinite worth. The narratives we tell ourselves beat us down.

They bring out the negative when what we need is a whole picture of our good, bad, and ugly. Mindfulness does not chase away our missteps or problems. It simply teaches us that we are whole, important, and unique beings just as we are.

Mindfulness helps us to get in touch with a full range of emotions. Think of your capacity for emotions, thoughts, feelings, and sensitivities. It's huge. We can experience the lowest of lows and the highest of highs in a matter of minutes, even seconds. Your whole and entire being consists of complexities that experts have been studying and will continue to study forever.

Understanding and believing your complexity will help unlock the assurance that nothing is a mistake. You are whole even when you feel you are lacking something. Everything you need is at your fingertips. What's surprising, and what many people take years to figure out, is that the more you pour out for others, the more whole you feel.

What you give is what you get. Mindful days keep our focus on our intrinsic worth and value in all its complexity, and that is something that will allow the negativity to fall away like fat off the bone.

Beginner's mind

One way to cultivate a beginner's mind and develop healthier thinking patterns is to stay curious. Instead of immediately beating ourselves up for negative thoughts and behaviors, we could ask questions instead.

Let's say you go to attend a meeting at work or at your child's school. Someone in charge says something that makes you angry. The best approach would be to dig into that feeling. You can ask yourself, "Why am I feeling this way?"

Explore with curiosity instead of targeted and intense negativity. Think about the situation from a beginner's perspective. What if this was my first meeting, and I knew little about the principal or the executive? How would I process the experience then?

This may seem overwhelming, but the goal is to disarm yourself. Take away the weapons that are hurting you. If you have so much going on in your mind that you can't separate things from each other, it may be time to step back and put on a fresh pair of glasses.

Liz Forkin Bohannon talks about curiosity in her book, Beginner's Pluck. She says that curiosity will more likely make you more successful as you ask yourself questions instead of making declarative statements.

With questions, we are in an open posture and ready to learn and change. Having a beginner's mind is about being open and willing to change, so curiosity helps us with this.

She also says that asking questions will dig deep into why you are doing what you are doing and will also help you evaluate your passion in the first place. It motivates you to make a change. You want things to turn out better, so you have to tweak how you have done things in the past to change the outcome.

As we ask ourselves questions and remain curious, we will solve our own problems in a much more positive way. The next time you face a brick wall (before you get too discouraged), click on the lightbulb of curiosity.

Brainstorm the ways you have handled this before and think about what you can do differently. Make a small adjustment and try again. Don't beat yourself up about the past. Simply switch something up to see if it makes a difference.

Nothing wrong with thinking

One assumption about mindfulness is that to do it right, you have to turn off your mind completely. Many people find that extremely difficult, so they feel like failures right off the bat. It's hard to sit still, pay attention, and organize our thoughts.

But it is a myth that we should turn our brains completely off while we practice mindfulness. Our mind is not evil. We don't need to run away from it. The goal is simply to pay attention to our thoughts.

It's important to circle back to the attitudinal foundation of non-judging. These thoughts that come into our minds should be considered but not judged. We don't have to criticize ourselves for having these thoughts. It's like we are tasting a new fruit for the first time, and many thoughts jump up as the sensation of the fruit slides around in our mouths.

The taste buds are telling us something. We can embrace curiosity and explore this new experience without judging our thoughts. If we don't like it, ask why. Is it bitter? Too hard or too soft? Is it similar to anything else we eat? Is the texture or smell throwing us off? Why?

We can train our minds, much like we train a new pet. It takes practice, dedication, and awareness. There are unwanted thoughts that will come in, and we have to lead and gently guide them away from us and replace them with new thoughts that are true and helpful. In order to go in the direction, we want, we have to sit with our thoughts first. We cannot ignore them or treat them harshly before we even have a chance to figure out what they mean.

It may be easier in mindfulness to notice the surrounding things externally. The breeze outside, the sound of a family chatting as they walk past you, or birds flitting around on a spring day.

You can focus on your breath and simply take in your surroundings. It is more of a challenge to be mindful internally. Thoughts feel so invasive, so abrupt, that it can be a struggle to weigh them.

Begin with the idea that your thoughts are not here to harm you, but they are here to teach you something, and that is why we want to pay attention.

Befriending our thinking

If we don't establish our thoughts as the enemy, it's a natural next step to befriend our thinking as we practice mindfulness. These thoughts are, after all, part of who you are.

They may need adjustments, but we can approach them with gentleness and kindness to let down our guard a little bit. Defensiveness will not help us move forward with our goals and dreams.

Draw close to your thoughts and approach them like an old friend. Using curiosity, ask the questions softly as we are learning to treat our thoughts kindly and with sensitivity. Mindfulness is about observing and non-judging, so we want to treat our thoughts with a generous attitude.

If you are in the middle of a mindfulness exercise when your mind wanders, try not to have a negative reaction to your mind as if it has done something wrong. Figure out why your mind wandered. Get to the root of the issue.

Work on coordinating parts of your mind; like your thoughts, emotions, and then actions. Find out how they are connected and why your mind works the way it does. It sounds complicated, but the work is worth it.

Focus on the present moment

As we approach our thoughts with kindness, we can let go of the past and the future. The best part of mindfulness is that it focuses on the present. What a beautiful way to live this life, moment by moment.

As we pay attention to the thoughts and emotions we have, it's easy to jump to conclusions or want to change things immediately. But patience is key to staying in the moment. What can we learn right now by paying attention to what is right in front of our faces? Friends, the possibilities are endless.

We spend much of our life planning for tomorrow. We have retirement plans, work goals, family vacation ideas, and physical fitness aspirations. Most people are, sadly, not satisfied with their current state of life. Society is always pushing us into the next day before we have juiced today for all its worth.

Gratitude can help us stay in the present and bring our perspective back to what we have been given instead of what we want to happen in the future or what we want to change about our lives. A gratitude journal is a wonderful mindfulness exercise because it keeps your eyes on the now.

Your gratitude journal can be a thick notebook with gold-lined paper, or the back of the grocery list from this morning's errands. Sit down with a pen and as you take deep breaths, list a few things from the last 24 hours that you are grateful for. I like to keep a short time frame because it helps to keep us in the moment.

We can look around and see the things that make us happy. It can be a small thing, like the simple breakfast you enjoyed, your favorite house plant, or the way the light falls into your living room at sunset.

Or it can be people that bring you great joy. Think about a few key moments in the last day that filled your heart with peace. Embrace the tiny bits of love that fill you up and give you the strength to keep going.

The present is a gift. It sounds cliche, but it is foundational to mindfulness. When we rush through this life, the people around us reach out to touch us, but we are already gone. How important it is to be present to ourselves, those we love, and the beautiful world we live in.

Now is always the right time

As we live in the present moment, the reasons to wait for change start mounting up. There are always so many things to change that it's easy to get frozen and have "analysis paralysis." When this happens, we push off taking action by analyzing all the reasons it's just not the perfect time.

It will never be the perfect time, so that makes it the perfect time!

If you wait too long to make a change for what you feel passionate about, the passion will wear off, and it will be hard to gain momentum. Start with being mindful of your goals and think about the next logical next step.

Go for a walk outside and, as you breathe and admire your surroundings, focus on one goal you think you can tackle. Clear away any judgment or negative self-talk and decide on one or two action steps you could take right away: like today. Don't wait.

We can get in our own way of success and progress by convincing ourselves that things will just get better. Or our problems will go away on their own. It can be tempting to take the easy way out and do nothing.

But being mindful demands honesty, and being honest with ourselves will lead us to those next steps. We can have the confidence and courage to take those next steps by using the attitudinal foundations discussed here.

"The present moment is the only time over which we have dominion."

-Thích Nhất Hạnh

What a beautiful way to view our life, especially those who are recovering control freaks. We have the present moment, but we cannot control the future. There are, in fact, many things that are beyond our control.

Mindfulness is not about control. It's about releasing and letting go of control. But that doesn't mean we should ignore the stewardship placed before us. The time we have been given is meant to be used.

Trapped in the past or living in the present

One Harvard study discovered that we spend nearly half of our awake time with a wandering mind, dwelling on either the past or the future.

Wow. Half of our awake time. That sounds about right. We think about our past often, trying to avoid pitfalls or heal from experiences. And some of us tend to live in the future, planning and scheming and hoping and daydreaming about what is coming.

So how do we move on from the past? How do we get "unstuck" from what has been dragging us down?

The past is incredibly powerful, as we can view things in hindsight. Events and circumstances are over, for good or bad, and we can study them with clear eyes. The problem is our emotions are usually involved at such a deep level that we revisit the past over and over like a torture chamber. Parts of us know how crucial it is to be free from our past, but it's addicting to go over scenes and feelings again and again.

If you have suffered trauma in your past, counseling and therapy can be a tremendous help. Licensed therapists are equipped with tools and methods to guide you to a better place mentally, emotionally, and physically. There is absolutely no shame in getting help if you are finding yourself deeply rooted in past events that are crippling your present life.

Therapy can be incredibly painful. It may feel sometimes like your heart is being ripped out of your body. It's also a big commitment and can sometimes take years to work through all the issues. Many would attest that it is beyond worth it. Opening yourself to true healing can set you on a trajectory toward a full life.

We have experienced haunting things in our past that we must overcome to live in the present. Many people struggle to move on and embrace their current life when they have heavy and traumatizing photos from their past on repeat in their minds.

After you get help to heal from your past, you can use the mindfulness practice of acceptance to embrace who you are, including your past. Whether it is painful memories because of your choices or others' choices forced upon you, accepting your reality is key to a whole and healthy life.

How To Stay In The Present Moment

Living in the present has become a necessity in this busy world, and most of us don't know how to live in the present; Here, we have listed a few ways to help you start the process.

Focus On Your Body

The first way to be in the moment is to focus on your body. Be more in tune with all the physical sensations you feel through your body in the present moment. Also, try to listen to and take care of your body's needs. Try to concentrate from head to toe and silently listen to your body.

Start your day right!

We are all constantly in a hurry at times in life; Instead of waking up in a terrible state and jumping out of bed, why not take some time for yourself when you wake up? Take a deep breath and try to focus on yourself and your surroundings.

Don't forget to take a few minutes out of your schedule and practice mindfulness. It can help you stay in the moment.

Conduct a conscious body scan.

One of the most helpful mindfulness exercises you can do is body scanning, which can help you to live in the present moment.

The procedure:

- Lie still on your back.

- Try some deep breathing exercises to become aware of your body.

- Be aware of your body; Try to focus on how your clothes feel on your body and how small things feel in contact with you.

- Try to focus on the parts of your body that hurt you.
  Focus on every part of your body, from your toes to your head.

Write a journal

Journaling is an excellent technique for learning to stay in the moment and is also one of the most popular mental health activities.American author Julia Cameron uses one of the journaling techniques called "morning pages."

Before heading to your workspace, take a few minutes to open your journal and start writing. There's no wrong way to write the morning pages. All you have to do is write three journal pages; without overthinking, write down everything that comes to your mind.This is just one way to keep a journal; You can opt for various other techniques, including log prompts and others.

Start single-tasking

It's easy to burn out when you multitask, which affects your overall performance and the quality of your work.

A single task helps you to work more efficiently. It can help you focus on yourself and be more present. Try to set up a single task in your life, not only when you work but also when you do small things like watching TV, focus on the TV instead of using your phone simultaneously.

Concentrate on your breathing.

Staying focused and controlling your breathing is one of the most important parts of meditation, which helps you to stay in the present moment.

Focus entirely on your breathing and do this while closing your eyes and sitting in the lotus position for better concentration. Feel the air flowing into your body and the air flowing out with every breath. Better focus and attention can also help quiet your mind and give you peace.

Focus on what's in front of you.

Most of us wander off while talking to someone or even reading or watching something. Focus on what's happening in front of you instead of drifting off into an imaginary world.

Practice mindful meditation

Mindful meditation is one of the most popular ways to learn to stay in the present moment and become more grateful, maintain peace of mind, and manage anger. In mental health development activities, meditation plays a significant role. It helps increase mindfulness by increasing focus and calm within us. Consider taking time out of your busy schedule to try to meditate; You can try to focus on the word "now" during meditation.

Spend time in nature

Spending time in the presence of the beauty of nature is one way to learn to be in the present moment effectively. Walking outside helps you focus better on your life, and walking also helps reduce your stress and anxiety by releasing endorphins.

Reduce your input

Sometimes we overload ourselves with a lot of work and focus on a million things. In such cases, it may make sense to shorten your contribution.

Instead of checking your email or social media as soon as you wake up, reduce your input, and focus on what's happening around you. Also, don't overexert yourself at work; keep your mind free of clutter. This habit can help you become mindful in your daily life.

Try chanting mantras

Singing mantras are commonly used in meditation to increase focus and learn to stay in the present moment. You can chant multiple mantras, as every culture and place has mantras in its language.

Try sitting in the lotus posture and chant your mantra. This simple procedure will help quiet your mind, reduce stress and anxiety, and focus on the present moment.

Try doing yoga

One of the many great tools to ground yourself is yoga! Yoga consists of the most versatile exercises with hundreds of benefits. It helps people suffering from depression and other mental illnesses. Yoga also allows you to feel yourself and your body and to connect them to the present moment. Yoga also helps you learn to be in the present moment by focusing on your breath and mind.

There are many yoga poses that you can do; Even if you are new to yoga, there are simple yoga poses like

Sukhasana, Vajrasana, and others that can help you get started.

Enjoy where you are

Each of us wants to build a better future, and there is nothing wrong with that, but in building your future, don't break down your present. According to Eckhart Tolle, "Expectation is more of a state of mind than a situation we find ourselves in," meaning that if we want to achieve something in life, we must wait for it. Still, on the contrary, it depends entirely on what we want to perceive.

For example, ask someone sitting at the bus stop what they are doing. Most of the time, they will reply that they are waiting for the bus, but what if, instead, they respond that they are sitting and breathing the fresh air and watching what is happening around them? Here you can understand the difference between two perceptions and how it affects our lives.

By simply changing your thoughts, you can start appreciating the present more. To know how to be in the present moment, we must first value and enjoy the present for what it is.

As Buddha said, "Don't dwell on the past, don't dream of the future, focus your mind on the present moment." What matters most is whether you live your life or are just passing by.

Set Intentions

Mindfulness requires a bit of planning. Like anything, you will not have success or progress overnight with just a snap of your fingers. If you are a routine person, setting an intentional time of the day to practice mindfulness will help you build up the new habit.

- You could take a walk after work every day, by yourself or with pets or family members. Pay attention to what's going on around you.

- Grab the gratitude journal we mentioned earlier and jot down a few things in the morning or at night. Keep it by your bed so that you can start your morning and end your day on a positive note.

- Use your planner to set goals. Each week, think about one way you can be more mindful. Maybe that's setting aside electronics during lunch or dinner and choosing to focus on your meal. Or not listening to music or anything on your commute. Set an alarm on your phone for once a day or even once an hour to take short breaks to just breathe and recenter yourself.

- Schedule a larger, longer set of time once in a while for a mindfulness retreat, project, or event. This could be a time of painting or art endeavor, even if you are not an artist. Or a morning to stay in bed journaling, reading, and resting. Everyone needs a mental health break every once in a while!

Using the foundation of non-judging, set reasonable intentions, and don't be afraid when you don't quite get it right. Mindfulness is practicing a way of life, and there is so much room to grow. You can take baby steps now, and with time you will see that you have made significant progress.

Kendra Adachi writes in "The Lazy Genius Way" that she set a goal of doing yoga every day to improve her mindfulness and flexibility. But when the goal was too big, she failed. So instead, she took the incredibly brave approach of setting the world's tiniest goal.

Starting on January 1st, she decided to do one yoga position every day. It was the downward dog pose. It took her seconds, but some days she even managed to do it twice! Because her goal was too small to quit, she spent the year and beyond doing yoga every day and has noticed the small change really improved her well-being.

Your intentions do not have to be huge. In fact, it's probably better if they aren't. You know yourself, so choose something manageable for you at this stage of your life.

Spend time with thoughts and feelings

Everyone knows relationships grow when you spend quality time together. You can't get to know a person unless you are talking and sharing, opening up in vulnerability, and being honest with each other.

It's the same way with ourselves. We have to spend time with our thoughts and feelings to get to know them, and through that, we can stay in touch with ourselves. Just like a relationship, we cannot ignore ourselves and expect to grow.

As we live a mindful life, we are going to come across thoughts and feelings that are uncomfortable, especially with our past and how we feel about events that happened years ago.

It's important in these moments to lean into the hard. Good things will come from a little bit of digging. It will take time and courage, but the more time you devote to this important work, the more it will help you in the long run.

Don't be afraid to take yourself out for coffee and dive into what makes you tick, what ticks you off, what you want out of life, and how you can make it happen. Ask yourself the hard questions and use the tools we have discussed to gain a better perspective and make an action plan.

Therapy can also help immensely with the complicated thoughts and feelings that arise. Sometimes it's vital to get an unbiased third party to weigh in on our most challenging circumstances.

There are conclusions that we might not have access to unless, with vulnerability, we invite someone else to peer into our life circumstances and advise with love. It doesn't even have to be formal therapy. A good friend who knows us well might help us see from a different viewpoint.

After you speak with someone, make sure to come back to yourself and sort out your thoughts and emotions again. Journal or do a walking meditation to open yourself up. Breathe deeply physically, but also give your body space to breathe metaphorically too. If you keep rushing through life, your thoughts and feelings may not get the space they need. And you don't want to lose touch and move too quickly to the next thing without addressing what's going on deep in your heart.

What does liberation from suffering mean?

Humanity is full of suffering. To be human is to suffer in one way or another. Some humans have endured more suffering than any human should ever be subjected to. It will break your heart.

Accepting pain and suffering is to become liberated from its effects. Yes, we will suffer and struggle throughout this life. Pushing pain and suffering away and ignoring or stifling it will not help us deal with it.

Part of the freedom that comes with mindfulness is allowing yourself to embrace your struggles. You don't have to want them or even like them but try not to turn your head away.

Self-compassion is a beautiful way to deal with the pain and suffering that has come across in your life. Not only are you acknowledging the difficult place that you find yourself in, but you are breathing life and hope into the situation instead of negativity. Have grace with yourself. Have patience with yourself. Talk to your own heart as if you were comforting a child.

Liberation from suffering does not mean that the pain and suffering will go away forever. It just means that you don't have to live in the prison of it. By accepting it, you are being true to yourself, and that gives you freedom.

Liberation is in the practice itself

Imagine being on top of a cliff and looking out at the land below. The sky feels the biggest you have ever felt in your life, and beauty surrounds you. The trees and their leaves, the wispy clouds in the sky, and the kiss of the wind on your face captures your attention.

You are there with all that makes you, you. Inside your body might be physical pain, or inside your heart might be brokenness that you aren't sure will ever heal. You are carrying weights, and you want to be free.

Close your eyes and raise your hands up in the air. Release the weight. Let it go. Accept who you are in all its beauty and uniqueness.

Be liberated.

Chapter 3: Awareness

Do you think that something as simple as awareness can unlock mindfulness for you? As you are learning about mindfulness, you might hear a lot about being aware.

Imagine you are experiencing a loss of a relationship. It could be a breakup, a friend that moved away, or a death. In your moments of shock and grief and passing through different stages, how aware are you of what's going on?

Are you in touch with how your body feels and how each emotion feels as they flood you throughout the day and night?

Awareness allows you, in the midst of pain, to experience pain differently. Freedom comes with awareness because you are learning about yourself and recognizing what your heart, body and soul may be going through.

We are so used to flying past our feelings, explaining them away, or doing our best to fix them immediately. However, if we are alert to pain as it comes up, we can peer with wisdom into our present circumstances.

Awareness will not take away our pain. If you have suffered a loss of a relationship; your emotions are deep and layered. You are not immune to pain just because you are highly self-aware.

You can choose small ways to bring awareness into your life as you are getting to know what it is. Living life in this way allows us to live with greater openness.

We live most of our lives on autopilot, doing the same things over and over without really thinking about it. We easily jump out of the present moment, and this breeds dissatisfaction. As you practice focusing on one thing at a time, you will increase your mindfulness and awareness.

It may be frustrating to remind yourself after you feel the familiar slide to pop back into awareness. Be gentle and kind, slowly shifting your mind back to the present. Look. Feel. Be. Check in with yourself, and with time, your ability to stretch out your awake moments will grow stronger.

Think of awareness as an outside force. It's not the same as thinking and feeling. It lies beyond that border. Awareness holds and contains your thoughts and feelings, but it does not control them.

Don't try to change everything that awareness is holding. You can watch your thoughts and feelings without being sucked into the swirl of them like the violent storm they can sometimes be. Create separation.

A Place to Sit by Kabir

Don't go outside your house to see flowers. My friend, don't bother with that excursion.

Inside your body there are flowers. One flower has a thousand petals.

That will do for a place to sit. Sitting there you will have a glimpse of beauty inside the body and out of it, before gardens and after gardens.

This poem by Kabir is a beautiful representation of how much potential we have inside of us waiting to be unearthed. Think about the flowers and petals that you hold within you, alongside all the complicated thoughts and feelings. Awareness holds onto everything so that you can tend to yourself like a garden.

Inhabiting awareness

We all know that worrying does not change our circumstances. So why do we do it? Why do we so desperately need control that we have convinced ourselves that worrying about something is worth our time?

It's easy to say that we shouldn't worry or even tell others not to worry, but yet the minutes and hours we spend on things we can't control is baffling.

If we could inhabit awareness, making it a part of our daily life, then we leave no room for worry. If awareness is a container that holds our thoughts and feelings, then we can gently nudge worry out of the way so that it doesn't enter the container.

All we have is the moment we are in. No one is guaranteed even their next breath. So, each breath then can be considered a miracle, a blessing, a chance to be grateful. We are so often taking even our very breath for granted.

So how do you inhabit awareness in your life? How can you make it a practice and habit that works with your lifestyle?

The first goal is to be awake. That sounds silly; of course, you are awake. But many zombies through life as if they are sleeping, and that will not lead to a fulfilling life. Awake yourself to what is going on in and around you. With careful mindfulness, consider the thoughts and feelings you hold in your awareness container.

Some thoughts or feelings may be very painful to you. Other thoughts are things you have been pushing away. Being awake is living with eyes wide open to what your life means. It means carefully considering what has happened in the past without judgment.

If something is too painful, acknowledge that and circle back to it later. But don't fall asleep to it, thus ignoring the problem. With time, you can summon the courage to confront the scariest parts of yourself or your past.

The second goal is to inhabit your body. Allow awareness to circle through your physical body and pay attention to what rises to the surface. Tensions can lie in the shoulders, stomach, back, or head. Focus and hold on to what your body is trying to tell you.

Too often, we ignore what our body is trying to tell us because we have become so used to the vessels, we have lived in for so many years. Sometimes our bodies are shouting at us, and it's important to pay attention. You can't inhabit awareness in your mental life if you aren't aware of the vital signs your physical body is giving.

The third goal is to remove distractions. Many things want our attention, but we want to be aware and in control. How would you feel if something terrible happened because you weren't paying attention? It may plague you with guilt as you realize you could have avoided it.

Think about how many times each day you are distracted, multi-tasking, and focused on more than one thing. At work or at home, it can be detrimental, and our performance will decrease if we can't stay focused.

Relationships also need quality time, and when we are pulled in too many directions, it can cause tension and frustration. With practice, we can stay aware and awake in each situation, each relationship, and every circumstance of the day.

Taking care of this moment

This moment is a gift, and you should never ignore it. As you look back on your life, think about moments or relationships you took for granted while you were in them. Have you lost someone that meant something to you? Do you regret the time spent with them, even if it was hard? Of course not. A life full of relationships is complex, and it will be better to treat each moment like a precious gift to be cherished instead of like a disposable item to be used, thrown away, and promptly forgotten.

Inner body awareness

What is the inner body?

The term "inner body" describes a flow of life that nourishes your physical being. As you gain insight into its space, you connect to the source of creation. In short, inhabiting your inner body slows the pace of your mind and brings mental and emotional balance.

Your inner body is the formless, non-physical part of you. It has no boundary and is located under the outer regions of your body. This power brings your physical self to life. Here you can feel the energy flowing within the confines of your skin.

Tune into this feeling and align with your inner body. To illustrate, imagine charging a phone. Watch as it comes to life and completes its tasks. Life energy works in the same way in your body. In this analogy, the phone is your body, and the electric current is its power. Once you can feel this subtle energy, your awareness increases, this goal is the result of connecting with your inner body.

Your physical body is an organic machine containing many systems and levels. Each of these occurs in different layers. Their surface includes skin, muscles, and bones. There are cells, fluids, tissues, and organs at a deeper level. Thought and emotion explain the subtler levels of form. Each of these layers forms the overall profile of your body.

Explore their nature and sense how they feel. This form of examination puts you more in touch with the inner body. As a result, your mind becomes a wise and helpful tool, and its movement cannot overwhelm you.

In reality, conscious space creates and holds every object in the cosmos. To accomplish this purpose, it works through all of your cells. This intellect is the inner body that works on your human level. When you tune into this, your mind and emotions come into balance.

What happens when you feel the inner body?

When you feel your inner body, its energy is activated. This action strengthens your body's life force, which nourishes everything at the cellular level. That's because you recover faster, don't age as quickly, and have fewer diseases.

Your body is an intelligent machine that has the power to regenerate and heal itself. It happens through the cooperation of many tissues, fluids, and cells. Each of these entities in your body is a conscious and wise being.

They use their minds to connect and work with many other systems. This act needs both attention and nutrients to survive and thrive. Without such awareness, your bodily features deteriorate. It is then difficult for them to heal.

When you become aware of your inner body, you bring awareness into your cells. It prevents unwanted thoughts and illnesses from accumulating in your space. Let's take the case of an owner who leaves his house to show how this works. What happens to their house if they don't return after a few years?

Dirt and debris are likely to build up in its walls. The building soon falls into disrepair, and uninvited guests invade.

Otherwise, intruders and debris are less likely to enter when someone is home. It keeps the house solid and intact. Likewise, as you connect with the inner body, your level of consciousness increases.

A higher level of consciousness creates space for the healing of the brain and body. In fact, your cells are becoming more spacious and in a state of equilibrium.

This action prevents excess mental energy and toxins from building up in your body. You will soon discover ways to improve your life and health. The result is less disease in the brain, body, and spirit.

How does the connection with the inner body affect your mind?

Connecting with the inner body strengthens, expands, and opens your mind. This awareness allows you to communicate with the space and wisdom of life. You gain inner strength, well-being, ideas, and solutions.

The dimension of space and knowledge is present in you. These enable your entire being to live with ease and balance. Believing that you are your thoughts blocks access to that intelligence. By merging with the inner body, you learn to see beyond the outer crust of your mind. This vision removes all mental blocks blocking space and knowledge within you.

A solid foundation of consciousness ensures that your thoughts and actions are not harmful to your well-being. Imagine building a tower on a flat base of loose sand. The tower won't stay there for long. Now imagine the same structure built on a stable, deep concrete base. The building remains stable – regardless of ground changes or weather conditions.

In this example, the tower shows your thoughts; its base is your inner body. A solid grounding in this base allows for a strong inner strength, well-being, and a greater awareness of life.

An alert and steady mind develop as you become more aware of your inner body. From that moment on, nothing gets past you, no matter what happens. When you dwell in this stillness, insight and inspiration arise. You then connect to the source of creation and realize that life is one. This insight comes when you connect with your inner body.

How do you practice inner body awareness?

You train to be aware of your inner body by being still first. It is then easy to feel your feelings and emotions. See if you can feel life beneath your skin. As you spend 3-4 weeks in this practice, thoughts will have less power over you as your awareness increases.

The following steps will help you become more aware of your inner energy field. It is essential to realize that they are clues and act as guides. With this intention, there are no rules when practicing. It helps to try each trick and find the one that works best.

Sit relaxed.

Sit and make yourself comfortable on the surface or in a chair you are resting on. When you are ready, close your eyes. There is no need to hold yourself in a rigid posture. The most important thing is that you use the least amount of effort to support your posture.

Remain as calm as possible.

A restless body reflects a hectic mind. When you keep your body still, the mind becomes less noisy. It becomes more aware of this practice. In addition, a stable body requires the brain to slow down the speed of its thoughts.

Watch your breathing.

If you find it easy, bring your attention to the movement of the breath. Start by taking a deep breath in and softening your focus as you exhale. When it is difficult to focus, imagine a bright healing light surrounding you. With each breath, visualize the breath in this light. Allow this light to fill all your space.

Take care of your chest cavity as it fills with air and the lungs empty. As you exhale, relax your efforts to control your breathing.

Become aware of the sensations in your body.

You will feel light and subtle sensations as soon as the body relaxes. These include slight tingling, tension, pain, and warmth in different places. Observe a gentle electrical sensation in your limbs and brain.

Here is a light and nourishing energy that beats your heart at the same time. Notice how the blood moves and flows from the center of your heart through your torso. This act of observation allows your body to relax.

Draw attention to your body, neck, and head.

Now that you are in tune with the body, explore each part. Start with your toes. Spend ten seconds on each and note how you feel. Feel your feet, legs, torso, neck, arms, and fingers. Then direct your attention to your whole being. Appreciate all reactions moving through your space. Recognize the vitality and presence that bring your form to life.

The mind will try to distract you with this exercise. As this happens, notice all the thoughts and questions that come to the surface. Keep returning to your focus point whenever you see this happening. Don't worry if you find it difficult to concentrate during this exercise. Understand that this is a short-term exercise to increase your awareness. Because of this, you don't have to force yourself to be perfect.

Notice the energy your body is holding.

Imagine your body is a hollow vessel. Is it easy or difficult? Stay with that awareness and explore it with your senses. You will soon feel the subtle energy in and around your skin. Continue with this feeling as long as you feel comfortable.

How can the method of inner body awareness be summarized?

To summarize, the method of noticing your inner body: be still, relax, and then observe your sensations and senses. When your mind wanders, please bring it back to your focus point. This exercise will help you develop a more intelligent mind and a healthy body. With this foundation, you can effortlessly let go of unwanted thoughts.

Do wisdom and consciousness exist in the body?

Every cell, tissue, and fluid in your body has wisdom and consciousness. These qualities thrive beyond the confines of your skin. The practice of being with your body opens the door to this idea. Such quiet wisdom sustains and animates all that exists. See its effect in nature, where the scope of life is infinite. As soon as you feel this movement, your whole life changes.

Every cell in your body is connected to all life energy. Within you, this vision is waiting to grow and blossom. To realize this, spend several minutes a day noting this power. Understand how it brings your body to life. By doing so, you awaken inner wisdom and grow as a person.

This movement changes your mind, your health, and your life. Soon you will have an enduring connection with the intellect of life. You will reach this goal after a few weeks of practice. From there, you can finish the awareness exercises and begin to release your mind. In short, this version changes your whole life.

Chapter 4: Anchoring

Mindfulness anchoring techniques; Anchoring body to stay present all the time

Mindfulness uses many techniques, and one of them is called anchoring. Anchoring allows us to check in on ourselves and stabilize. Anchoring encourages you to stay present at all times.

Anchoring is about focusing your attention on just one thing. If you become distracted, you can redirect your mind back to that one thing. Often our mind wanders because its job is to fire ideas at such a fast speed that we can't ever keep up.

So just like dog trainers use consistent methods to teach the animals to listen and obey, we can consistently and kindly anchor ourselves to build that muscle memory.

Why is it important to stay present? Regret comes from not living our life to the fullest, and many suffer from regret. The best gift we can give to ourselves is to pay attention to the present moment and not run away from it.

All of nature lives in the moment. The trees, the ocean, the animals. We can learn a lot from them, as we should. Children also have a way of not worrying about the future but living more carefree lives. What if we fully embraced the present for what it is without wishing it away?

There are many ways to anchor yourself in order to stay present. Breath is the most common way to anchor oneself. It is with you all the time, it is natural, and involves movement. What's also great about breathwork is that it is something tangible to which you can hold on.

You can place your hands by your side, on your chest, or stomach. Our breath can often become shallow and too much in the upper chest. The goal is to teach ourselves to breathe with our belly. Deep breathing also combats the fight-or-flight response that surges when we feel threatened. It also fills the body with oxygen which we need to live.

When you stop what you are doing and focus on your breath, it will ground you. Involve all your senses; feeling, hearing, connecting to the rest of your body. Notice how your chest moves and your stomach fills up as you breathe in and deflates as you breathe out.

Breathing gives you another chance every few seconds when your mind wanders. It's a reminder that it's a practice, and you get to try again, and again, and again. Breathing deeply and focusing on that single act will help to calm you, regulate your emotions, and clear your mind of all the clutter.

If you want a specific technique when breathing, here are a few.

1. Box breathing is when you breathe in through your nose for four seconds, hold the breath for four seconds, breathe out through your mouth for four seconds.

2. Alternate nostril breathing: The first way you can do this is by holding your dominant hand like a fist underneath your nose. Use your thumb to close your right nostril and inhale. On the exhale, release your thumb and use the

knuckle of your index finger to close your left nostril.

The second way would be to rest your index and middle finger on your forehead between your eyebrows. Alternate your thumb and knuckle of your ring finger to close each nostril at a time while breathing deeply and exhaling.

3. Long exhale: Some might notice that it is easier to inhale longer than to exhale. Spend a few minutes focusing on the exhale, breathing out longer than you did before, and trying to empty every last breath before inhaling again.

Be careful not to push yourself. It's not healthy to try to achieve everything. This isn't about proving yourself or pushing the limits but focusing on your breath or an object to move toward mindfulness.

If you need to look at something, focus your eyes on one thing while doing a breathing exercise or close your eyes if you are feeling overstimulated. You can even combine breathing with mantras.

Anchoring with mantras empowers you with positive thoughts and grounds you to the truth. This is a fluid option you can use on the go to recenter yourself mentally.

Here are a few mantras that you can test out to find what works for you. "I am" statements give you control, but a mantra can be created with anything you want to affirm to yourself.

You can start them with: I can, I want, I will, I have, etc.

1. I am loved.
2. I don't need to chase anything.
3. I trust the process.
4. I am patient and kind.
5. I am where I need to be.
6. I am grateful.
7. I am free.
8. I am beautiful.
9. I am worth it.
10. I can grow and learn.

Sometimes one word can trigger you to settle down and feel connected with yourself. Love. Hope. Peace. Truth. Grateful. Heart. Family. Beauty. Safety. Patience. Now.

You can use the mantra to circle back to one thought as you practice mindfulness. Say it aloud or in your head. Combine this with breathing and connecting to yourself.

Connecting the mind and body is extremely important in mindfulness, so a body scan is one way to work through each component of what makes you, you.

When performing a body scan, you need an open mind and heart, just like anything else in your mindfulness journey. You are simply observing and bringing awareness to your physical body without judgment.

Emotions and thoughts will certainly come and may be overwhelming but use your body as an anchor and focus on the next part of the scan.

Either lying down or sitting, begin at the bottom of your body. This practice is used in Jon Kabat-Zinn's training program for mindfulness-based-stress-reduction which treats illnesses and chronic pain.

Start with your toes and foot on one side, and move up to your leg. The goal is to focus your mind on each part of your body, paying attention to what it might tell you. Focus for a few seconds, then move on through your mid-section, torso, and arms, and end with the face and head.

Allow memories to flood you as your mind discovers and explores each part of your body. Give appreciation where it is due, notice pain that cries out softly or loudly, and think about not just your physical heart but the experiences and emotions you often feel deeply in your heart.

It is useful to ground ourselves to the bodies we use every day for many purposes. A body scan can illuminate areas to which we have given little attention and recognize trouble spots. A shorter body scan, either lying down or sitting, is also useful.

If you don't want to commit to a whole-body scan, lying down and paying attention to your body for a few minutes can also help you relax. If you do this mindfulness exercise before or at bedtime, you might fall into a more relaxed sleep.

Target specific areas of your body that you want to focus on. If you suffer from headaches, neck pain, or back pain; try to relax those muscles by breathing in and out slowly and bringing deep peace to those areas.

Jon Kabat-Zinn says on page 153 of his book, *Wherever you go there you are,*

"We speak of broken hearts, of being hard-hearted or heavy-hearted, because the heart is known in our culture as the seat of our emotional life. The heart is also the seat of love, joy, and compassion, and such emotions are equally deserving of attention and of honoring as you discover them."

He encourages during the body scan and lying down mindfulness moments to recognize the body parts as physical but also metaphorical. What does the heart represent? Your throat and voice? Your gut? Not only do our bodies perform amazing, miraculous tasks every day, but some parts represent something deeper as well.

Morning time is a great way to anchor yourself and start your day out right. Though we are attached to sleep and require a good night's rest, even getting up a few minutes earlier in the morning can improve our mindfulness.

Greet the day without your phone, laptop, TV, or even the newspaper. Greet the DAY. The sun (if it is up yet), the still air, the quiet house, your quiet soul. Breathe deeply using one of your favorite techniques and wake your mind, body, and heart up to all the opportunities to come to you that day.

It's been proven over and over that gratitude and the appreciation of life itself does wonders for our mental health. There will be plenty to worry about as the day progresses, but in the morning, before the rush begins, take advantage of the time to anchor yourself.

"Morning is when I am awake and there is a dawn in me..." Henry David Thoreau, *Walden*

If you are a glass-half-full kind of person, you may already feel optimistic about what anchoring, and mindfulness can do for you. You may get excited about the positive benefits, but you might also have a hard time teaching yourself to relax.

With time, these exercises will grow on you, and you will choose your favorites. If you are a glass-half-empty kind of person, it might take more time to get used to living in the present and paying attention to what's going on in your body and mind. Stick with it. Don't give up.

Mindfulness brought to all the senses

Our five senses are an absolutely incredible way to participate in being human on this earth. Touch, smell, taste, sight, and hearing are beautiful gifts that allow us to connect with ourselves, with each other, and the world around us. Mindfulness takes advantage of the sensory experiences and gives us something to latch onto as we live wide awake and alert.

Have you ever pretended to be blind? When you were a child, did you close your eyes and practice walking around the house, bumping into furniture but also boasting about how well you know your way around?

If you were to lose one of the senses, it's obvious that all the other senses are heightened. For those who cannot see, their hearing becomes especially attuned. For those who cannot hear, their eyesight sharpens. For those who cannot taste, their sense of smell becomes more of a pleasure.

Mindfulness puts you in touch with each of your senses. Because you are paying more careful attention, you will notice sounds you never cared about before.

Or while you are eating, your tastebuds will light up in a more gratifying way now that you aren't distracted by one million things.

Here are some exercises for each sense.

Seeing: The Grand Canyon is so vast and unique that each time of the day offers a different view. The colors of the canyon change based on the position of the sun, clouds, and season. You also can experience the contours of color in a walk around your home.

Maybe the sights don't seem special, but they do change. Notice the trees, their leaves, and the way the wind blows through them. Look around at the people who you see every day or are complete strangers. Pay attention to any and all living things, from the tiniest of ants to the neighbor's pets.

If you kept a journal of observations from a routine walk, you might notice patterns and recurring themes. When you walk in the afternoons, what do you notice then that you don't see on your morning walk? If you go for a walk in the morning, pay attention to how you feel about the new day and what is on your mind.

What changes in an evening walk when the sun is setting, and indoor lights flicker on? Pay special attention to nature; a nearby pond or lake, the sunrise or sunset, the blooming flowers. Ordinary things come alive when you pay attention.

Hearing: If you have ever camped outside, you know how the forest and the wild come alive with noises when the sun goes down. Crickets, owls, coyotes, bugs, and birds of all shapes and sizes chatter endlessly. We struggle to find peace and quiet because it seems like this noisy world isn't ever truly shut down.

It's tricky to really hear things because we so often ignore them. The smallest of sounds, though, can put us in the present. Even if it is a busy road in the middle of a workday, the sounds of truck mufflers and motorcycles remind us we are not alone. What annoying or common sound can you appreciate today?

Touch: Studies show that babies who are just born desperately need touch in order to thrive. Touch is a basic part of being human that serves to comfort and soothe. Our skin is incredibly sensitive and just reaching out with bare fingers to touch something sends so many messages to our brains.

Maybe it has been a while since you walked barefoot. If you go outside, what do you feel walking on the grass or pavement with just your naked feet? Do you step more carefully? Are you tickled with sensation? Is it enjoyable or weird?

Be mindful of what you touch throughout the day and how it makes you feel. The thickness of an onion while you slice vegetables for dinner, or the face of someone you love. Listen to the tingles of your skin.

Smell: Have you ever borrowed clothes from someone else, and when you put them on, you recognized the smell? Whether it's the brand of cigarettes they smoke or perfume they wear, clothes often carry a distinct smell if worn often.

Food also carries a strong smell, which translates to memories for many people. A bakery with donuts might remind you of Saturday mornings with your dad. Or chicken curry brings up memories of dinners with a best friend.

What smells calm you, and what memories do powerful smells conjure up in you? Do you find yourself sickened by some smells and drawn to others?

As you go about your week, stop over a lit candle, a simmering pot on the stove, or a yard after a fresh mow. Connect the smells to memories and feelings and be mindful of how you can relish in the moment. Take the time to let the smells transport you.

Taste: Food is so much more than sustenance. It truly is an experience. Eating a meal is a wonderful way to experience mindfulness as you can devote your entire attention to focusing on what you are tasting at that moment.

We will go into this further, but for now, think about the last meal you ate today. What flavors do you remember? Were you paying attention? How often do you eat this meal, and does it bring you joy?

Because eating is part of our survival, it can become mundane. But opening our eyes to what the experience of a meal is can welcome a new layer of mindfulness.

Mindfulness of eating

One reason people encourage reading more in this day and age is because often we don't focus on one thing at a time. It has been mentioned previously that mindfulness is about focusing, paying attention, being aware, and being open to what is happening in and around us.

Reading a book invites a person into an immersive experience where they are only doing one thing. Unless you are listening to an audiobook, it is very difficult to read and do something else simultaneously.

Eating is the opposite. Many people eat while they are talking on the phone, watching a video, talking with others around a table, or even driving. Because we have to eat so many times each day, our meals have lost their luster and we don't focus on what we are eating and the experience of a meal.

Even if you have had a good meal recently, think about whether you were mindful while eating it. Reflect on what and how you ate and how you might be more mindful next time. These tips will help.

1. Start by thinking about why you chose this food for this meal and what it will do for your body. Evaluate your choices and ask yourself if you chose the food on autopilot or if you have reasons behind what you eat.

    Cost? A diet? Boredom or laziness? There is a reason, but you might not realize it until you think about it.

2. Savor each bite, eat slower, and express gratitude for the food. It's not healthy to eat quickly anyway, so slowing down is better for you physically and mentally.

   While you don't have to slow down so much that you take hours for your lunch break, slow down enough to pay attention.

3. Invite your senses to join in. Smell the food. Look at its textures and colors. Slowly blow on the food if it's hot and feel the way it jumps into your mouth. If you are drinking a smoothie or a cool drink, notice the cool sensation as the liquid goes down your throat and chills your chest.

   Listen to your fork hitting the plate and feel the tension in your fingers as you cut the meat. Tune into the unique sounds, smells, and feelings during your meal.

4. If you have a negative relationship with food, take back control of your eating habits. Just because people or marketing is pushing you to consume a certain type of food doesn't mean you have to indulge.

   Make decisions for your body that are healthy. Be honest, open, and non-judgmental toward yourself if you are struggling. Use mindfulness to plan your meals with as much affirmation and peacefulness as you can muster. Get support from friends and family to help you practice mindful eating.

5. Turn off distractions. If you can eat without TV, electronics, or even a book or magazine, you will be free to pay more attention to the eating experience. Respect the meal and treat it like the privilege it is.

    Of course, eating with friends and family can be an enjoyable experience, and they are not always distracting. But even in the company of others, you can focus on your food and the conversation while being fully present in the moment.

    One of the most beautiful parts of the human experience is sharing a meal with those you care about. Try to fully engage and say no to the temptation to check your phone or stare at your plate to avoid conversation.

If you have ever eaten while camping, hiking, biking, or doing some other strenuous activity, you know that the richness of the food is enhanced because your body so desperately needs it. Even a drink of water satisfies such an intense thirst that you forget it's just mere unflavored water.

This is not a suggestion to starve yourself in order for your food to taste better. But it is important to give your body healthy, delicious food and plenty of water to keep it satisfied. Some recommend smaller meals throughout the day. Others recommend plenty of healthy snacks instead of greasy, fatty food that won't do much for you in the long term.

Mindfulness at home, work, and in the world

Jon Kabat-Zinn says on page 86 of his book *Coming to our senses*:

"It is the challenge of this era to stay sane in an increasingly insane world. How are we ever going to do it if we are continually caught up in the chatter of our own minds and the bewilderment of feeling lost or isolated?

Ultimately, it is only love that can give us insight into what is real and what is important. And so, a radical act of love makes sense- love for life and for the emergence of one's truest self."

Staying sane in an insane world begins in the home, where you spend a lot of your time with whom you love. What does a radical act of love look like for you, and how would you create that in your home?

How can you show up for yourself and allow the roots of mindfulness to start at home and then branch out as you spend your days?

Walk around your house with a notebook and take notes about each room of the house. Are there certain parts of the house that make you cringe? If clutter is bothersome to you, where is it building up on countertops and desks?

As you look at each room, put on another set of lenses to help you view your space as either life-giving or draining.

Next, sit down with your notes and make a plan for turning your at-home living space into a simple yet beautiful place for you to feel calm. If you feel soothed by candlelight; set an alarm on your phone or put a sticky note on your refrigerator that reminds you to light candles. The best time might be in the evening after the sun goes down, after dinner. This small reward will give you a specific time of day to relax and unwind.

If you found some corners of your rooms particularly cluttered, schedule a few hours on the weekend to fill a trash bag with donation items. The clutter can affect us more than we know. A clean or decluttered room can do wonders for our mindset.

Show yourself some love. Light the candles. Declutter the rooms. Get rid of excess items that mean nothing to you and organize the paperwork on your counter into one folder or bin. Your sanity depends on it!

Walking

It seems strange to walk with no end in sight, but mindfulness while walking is the opposite of getting to a destination. Each step can put us squarely in the present time, and those who connect with physical activity might just fall in love with mindful walking.

Stress builds up in our bodies, and walking is one of the best ways we can channel that stress away from us in a healthy way.

Try to walk outside if the weather permits. Your landscape and views will change as you walk, giving you new things to which you can pay attention. Our tendency is going to tempt us to hurry, but the goal is to slow things down, just like mindful eating.

One challenge for yourself is to sync your breath and step cycle. This might require you to walk and breathe slower in order to stabilize the breathing, so it is not too quick. You may take multiple steps for a slow inhale, and multiple steps for a slow exhale. Count them if you need to, or just listen to the sound of your feet hitting the ground.

Think about your body as you walk. Are your shoulders raised with a confident pose, or are you slouching while you walk? Do you feel pains or aches anywhere? As you do your breathwork and use anchoring to keep you in the present, enjoy this activity as a full-body experience and not just for your legs.

Pay attention to your chest, the rhythm of your breathing, and your steps. Relax your stomach and shoulders, and maybe even close your eyes. Where do you feel most comfortable placing your hands? Try a few different varieties.

If you can establish a routine of walking mindfully, you may notice the benefits immediately. Not only is daily walking excellent for your health but putting effort into the exercise will allow you to be more mindful. If you usually listen to podcasts or music while you walk, or talk on the phone, take a break from that for the first week. Just walk.

Then you can add what you want but keep it simple. The goal is not to be distracted with multi-tasking, but to be present. There are many podcasts and streaming services that provide mindfulness exercises that you can listen to on the go. Being led through an exercise while you walk will help focus your mind on what you are doing and how your body feels.

One study shows us the benefit of mindful walking. Twenty-nine participants experienced mindful walking along the river Rhine for up to 10 days. The mapped yet unpaved route had obstacles. The participants were instructed to overcome as they came across them.

Once the study was completed, the data showed significant improvements in mindfulness skills as well as mood. Mindful walking had a positive effect on the participants. Even though the study measured a short amount of time, it stands to reason that mindful walking will improve your mental health and is worth a try.

Work and the world

Scott Shute is the founder of MWA: Mindful Workplace Alliance. The group consists of leaders from big companies like Google and Verizon. He is passionate about bringing mindfulness to work and is seeing success across the board. Many workplace environments can feel like a bomb just waiting to go off.

Emotions run high, feelings get hurt, and poor leadership can ruin a batch of new employees, no matter how qualified they are for the job. Shute is determined to reset the emotional pressure by using mindfulness practices to help employees handle difficult situations better.

One woman was a skeptic at first, but after a year of practicing mindfulness, she could get up in front of 80 people and give a presentation. When she got the butterflies before presenting, she engaged in breathwork and presented with a confidence that she had never had before. Leaders who invite this practice into their workplace are doing a great service to their employees, who might feel safer in an environment that acknowledges the stress of a busy schedule.

How would you bring mindfulness to work? Before you arrive, hopefully, you have already anchored yourself in the morning mindfulness routine. If not, take a minute or two and focus on your breathing, calm your spirit, and remind yourself to live in the present.

When work challenges erupt, always pause before responding or reacting harshly. Even just taking one or two seconds to gather yourself can help you stay present, patient, and calm. We all know what it is like to be disappointed in the workplace, so expect moments to come and be ready to anchor yourself again.

You may find yourself anchoring several times a day or maybe only once. Lunchtime is a good time to practice mindful eating instead of shoving down a sandwich while standing up and reviewing the project details your boss assigned you.

Take a break. Be aware of how you are pushing your body and check in with yourself. Walk up and down the stairs or around the office, or outside if you can. Be present with yourself, your co-workers, and the work itself.

Mindfulness will also help with focus while you are working. Deadlines can be stressful. Sometimes it feels overwhelming, and you might not think you will accomplish in time what needs to be done. Train your body and your mind to focus on the task at hand and set others aside. If technology is getting in the way and you can set that aside, it will help immensely. If everything feels important, narrow in on what you need to be working on, make the decision, and stay focused.

Stay present, and if you need a break to focus on your breath, plant your feet on the ground, close your eyes and anchor yourself again. Don't get embarrassed if you have to do this multiple times a day. This is good work you are doing.

Whether you are at home, at work, or out in the world on a Saturday afternoon enjoying the beautiful sunshine, take mindfulness with you. Think about your interactions with other people; strangers, as well as those you love. Who would benefit if you took an extra pause before saying a hurtful comment?

Everyone. You cannot be perfect. You are going to fail and make mistakes. But using mindfulness to train yourself to be kinder to your mental health will allow others around you to feel safe in your presence. What a beautiful gift that is for humanity.

If you are having trouble practicing your breathwork throughout the day, set a timer on your phone. It's been said that it takes a minimum of three weeks to create a habit.

For the first three weeks, you might need an external reminder. Set it at lunch so that you can remember to eat mindfully, whether at home or at work. Set your alarm clock earlier by just a few minutes so you can practice a morning routine. And set it at night to finish out the evening with breathwork, gratitude, and a little love for yourself and all the moments that day that you lived in the present moment.

Mindfulness of thoughts and emotions

Being mindful of our emotions means not casting them to the side. It means giving your emotions the dignity and honor they deserve as a place in your mind and body. We can learn to sit with our emotions and pay attention to what they have to tell us.

Do you believe every thought that comes into your head, especially when it is about you? Would you say the things you tell yourself aloud to a friend who you care about? Chances are, there is a lot of negative self-talk going on, and you may have been believing it for far too long.

Just because a thought or emotion comes into your mind and body doesn't mean it is true. Grounding ourselves in the moment will help to process thoughts and emotions in a non-threatening way. Use breathwork, a mantra, or check in with your senses for a moment to be fully in the present.

Meditation techniques

Jon Kabat-Zinn says on page 33 of his book, *Wherever you go there you are,*

"Meditation is not about feeling a certain way. It's about feeling the way you feel."

Practice meditation by sitting still on the floor or in a chair. Choose a time limit. Pay attention to your posture and your body. Decide on an object to focus on or simply focus on your breathing. The goal is not to ignore or judge your thoughts and feelings but to be aware of them.

Use the breathing techniques mentioned and be gentle with yourself as you focus on your breathing.

Feel your body from the inside out. Close your eyes and listen to what your body is telling you. Are your shoulders slouching? Is your back tight? Go back to focusing on your breathing while being aware of your body.

Placing your hands in different positions while meditating may be a tangible way to connect with the experience. Try placing them on your knees or in your lap. If you leave them palms up, does it make you feel more open? Explore different options.

Progressive muscle relaxation is a technique that focuses on tightening and then releasing your muscles. You can start at the top or bottom of your body and work your way through.

Tighten your muscles and hold for a few seconds before releasing. This may work through tension you have felt built up in various parts of your body; shoulders, back, hands or legs.

If you are having trouble doing meditation on your own, there are many free resources online to give you guided meditation exercises.

This may include a visual guide, such as a video, or an audio guide on a podcast. The music is soothing, and you can create a meditative experience from the comfort of your own home.

Shadow and Secondary Emotions

Dr. Claire Nicogossian talks about shadow emotions in her book *Mama, You are Enough*. After many years of meeting with women as a clinical psychologist, she explored the darker emotions women feel, such as disgust, anger, sadness, and anxiety. She teaches women how to acknowledge and deal with the negative emotions they come across while parenting.

Women, at times feel ashamed to talk about the troublesome parts of parenting because society paints a beautiful picture of the family. However, if the mother's negative emotions are not dealt with, that beautiful picture can become quite fractured and unhealthy.

What sort of emotions have you felt but have told no one about? Rage? Disappointment? Self-loathing? Inadequacy? Loneliness?

These shadow emotions are not meant to control us. We can learn self-control and patience through mindfulness. It's important to practice how to stay in control of our emotions. Too often, we let thoughts swirl around in our brains with no dumping zone. Being mindful requires us to first acknowledge the thoughts and then work through them.

One other thing to keep in mind is that you might be dealing with secondary emotions as well. Anger is known to be a secondary emotion, which means it is only revealed as a display, but something else deeper is going on.

For many people, it is easier to express anger and frustration than to feel sad or hurt. Because sadness and hurt make us feel vulnerable and weak, we use anger to cover up that like a shield around our true feelings. This is difficult to pinpoint because anger truly feels like its own strong emotion. But when you are feeling angry, sit with it for a moment and dig a little deeper. Find out what's hiding underneath your anger.

For example, someone who has recently been in a terrible car accident might be working hard in physical therapy. When the therapist pushes them to do an exercise over and over, the pain might trigger an angry response. The patient might throw something in anger or hit their fist on the table.

But soon after, tears fall, and the patient admits, "I just feel so helpless. How am I going to take care of my family if I can't even walk to the bathroom by myself?" Sadness, disappointment, unmet expectations, and feelings of helplessness crippled the patient because of the extensive injuries.

The first step for the patient is to feel the pain of the loss. Grieve the circumstances. Hear the inner voice that cries for a do-over. They will come back stronger and with more determination if they allow themself to feel the negative emotions first.

We can go back to what Brené Brown says about "the story I am telling myself." What are the thoughts forming in my mind and heart? What is the narrative being strung, and is that the truth?

If we are careful to consider our thoughts, we can be mindful of when we need to embrace them and when we need to work through them to a healthier place.

Remember, thoughts by themselves are neutral. The way they become positive or negative is what we attach to them. For example, we can say that it is windy outside. That is a neutral thought. It is just an observation about the weather.

If we follow up that thought with, "I can't sit outside on the porch for lunch," then we are feeling negative about it, and our mind goes down that track.

But if we lay the track for positive thought, like "I can still walk around the neighborhood while wearing a windbreaker jacket," then we are moving forward and staying in the moment without being too discouraged.

Mindfulness in relationships and communication

Throughout this book, we have been talking about how mindfulness applies to your life and particularly you personally. We have dug deep into what you can do to practice mindfulness. Our lives are not lived in a vacuum, though, so a huge part of mindfulness is going to be how we interact with others.

When you are on your own, you can control your breathing, set your routines, and enjoy a mindful walk. But the world is filled with relationships, both personal and professional, and learning to bring mindfulness into our conversations with others is crucial.

First, we can think about casual relationships that require our attention but don't hold our highest affection. Think co-workers, your boss, acquaintances from your yoga class, and the people you spend time with but don't get vulnerable and open with too often. How can we bring mindfulness into those spaces?

Respecting others is a great way to think the best about this world and treat others just like you want to be treated. This means to care about what they say even if you don't agree with them.

Listening respectfully and thinking the best about them, will help you maintain a positive outlook. When there is conflict in relationships, it is of utmost importance to remain calm. Leave the room briefly if you need to calm yourself down before speaking.

Practice your breathwork in the hall or the bathroom and regain your composure. The best way to handle sticky situations is not to give in to strong emotions in the heat of the moment. Count to ten and then back to zero to calm yourself down or repeat your mantras.

Your emotions are important and not to be ignored. Just like mentioned earlier, your thoughts and emotions need to be acknowledged and not stuffed away. But if you can tell that what you are feeling is about to take over your body, in order to avoid a big mistake, you must acknowledge them without acting upon them.

If you are at your workplace, keep it professional. If there are other people around, simply ask to speak in private with whoever is fueling the fire. Keep your tone even and give the person a chance to speak without your interruptions.

Remember respect. Even if the other person is not showing you the respect you think you deserve, in the moment you can offer them respect, and a fair conversation.

Second, everyone knows the blessing and curse of family life and extended family members. Just bring up a recent Christmas party, and there is sure to be a plethora of dramatic stories and mishaps.

Misunderstandings, arguments, disagreements, and hurt feelings come with the territory within small or large families.

Because these people are "your people" and will hopefully be for a very long time, you want to approach interactions with them as respectfully as possible but with a certain openness and privilege that you might not offer others.

Beware of toxic relationships because even if you are related to them, if your mental health is negatively affected regularly, it might be time to rethink how much they influence you and your decisions.

Mindfulness needs to be practiced in double doses when more family members are around, so don't skip your morning routine. If you get overcome with emotions, step aside or grab one of your family members that you have a good relationship with to talk. Being mindful of the situation means you can recognize when your thoughts and emotions are spiraling out of control.

Better yet, go for a walk to get away for a little while and reset. If you need to have an honest conversation with someone, bring in a third party to make sure things stay civilized. It's hard to find unbiased third parties when you are all family but do your best to have someone in the room with a level head. Listen to the other person, stay present in the moment, and try not to drag any drama into the conversation that doesn't need to be there. Keep it simple.

Last, romantic relationships are where most people have the most conflict. When you are in a long-term relationship, trust can be built over time and then destroyed in seconds.

This makes individuals feel vulnerable, even threatened at times. Because everyone argues in serious relationships, it's important to argue well.

How do you argue well? Psychologist John Gottman came up with The Four Horsemen of Conflict: Criticism, Contempt, Defensiveness, and Stonewalling.

Here are some tips on how to prevent them from ruining a relationship and how to remain mindful during an argument.

Criticism: Everyone knows how painful it feels when a person is verbally attacking you. The fight-or-flight response kicks in, and all you want to do is to protect and defend yourself. Communication often starts with this, turns into a fight, and both people are hurt with no solution.

Before you focus on the problem at hand, use "I" statements to express what you are feeling and thinking. This allows you to be mindful of your thoughts and emotions by acting on them rashly or taking out your negative emotions on the other person.

Don't accuse the other person unless you want them to put on their armor and defend themselves. Explain your pain and then invite the other person to explain their pain. You can even use Brené Brown's words and say, "The story I am telling myself is _____."

Contempt: This sounds like criticism but is less pointed. People use contempt to manipulate, twist words, act cruelly, and bully. Contempt can look like sarcasm, mocking, or disrespectful body language.

Before the argument gets heated or when your partner makes you want to roll your eyes and make fun of them, remind yourself of their good qualities. Don't give in to your temptation to be the "smarter" person. Humble yourself and stay in the moment. Try to understand their point of view.

Defensiveness: It's easy to play martyr and call yourself the victim. This can lead to manipulation by shifting the blame to the other person. It's natural to feel defensive when you and your partner are sharing difficult words. Can you let your vulnerability show, though?

Try to be open and accept that your partner is saying something for a reason. Let your hurt be there for a minute, and maybe even mention that what they are saying is hurtful. And if you need time to think about it, that's okay too. Take responsibility for your actions and lean into your partner's thoughts without judgment.

Stonewalling: This can also be known as the Silent Treatment. People withdraw to avoid conflict, and some can refuse to speak to their loved ones for a very long time. This is unhealthy because it doesn't resolve the problem.

It breeds bitterness and resentment, and those walls are hard to break down if it has been a long time. Don't let it get that far. If you struggle to get through the conversation and find that you very much want to ignore it, keep your mouth shut and run away, then it might be time to take a break. Communicate that you need to take a few breaths and think about what you feel.

Look your partner in the eye and give them a time in which you will return to the situation and resume communication. Do something soothing, but don't go too far. Your relationship is too important to ignore.

(Of course, these tips are assuming a relationship without a history of abuse. If you are being abused, seek professional help.)

Chapter 5: Dealing with setbacks

We have talked a lot about forward motion, but what about when something goes wrong in our mindfulness journey, and we feel like a failure? It could have been a conversation with someone you care about in which you very much wanted to be present but then got lost in the moment and said something hurtful.

Or maybe you wanted to start your morning routine as soon as your alarm went off, except the deadness of the night kept you in bed, hitting the snooze button. It's understandable to have set goals for yourself and then feel disappointed and frustrated with yourself or others when things don't turn out the way you wanted.

Mindfulness is forging a new path in your brain, and it involves cutting down thick weeds and high grass. Because you care enough about your mental health to try to stay in the moment, you are going to be tested. Remember to keep your goals small and doable. And if anything, begin the day with the goal and mindset to be at peace in the present. Whenever you think about it during the day, take a deep breath and remind yourself of the present.

Shefali Tsabary is a clinical psychologist in New York City. In her book, *The Awakened Family*, she tells a story of failing to meet her daughter in the present moment and regretting the harsh words exchanged. Her daughter was telling her about fashion, going on and on about certain types of clothes, new styles in a magazine, and beauty products. Dr. Shefali was flustered and too obsessed with her personal opinions on the topic that she shut her daughter down. She scolded her for focusing on superficial things instead of the more important things in life.

Dr. Shefali is entitled to her opinions, and as the mother, she was dying to share them with her twelve-year-old. But because she was focused on the future and didn't fully enter the present moment with her child, she missed the opportunity to have a pleasant conversation about harmless clothes and styles.

Dr. Shefali says on page 201, "How on earth was I going to reconnect and realign myself with the present moment?"

She apologized to her daughter and admitted feeling fearful about the future. Her daughter was honest and said, "Mom, you need to trust yourself.

You've taught me what matters and what doesn't." What a beautiful act of forgiveness. Dr. Shefali knew that despite that, she lost precious connection time with her daughter.

All the mindfulness professionals that have been doing this for ages still have to wake up and choose to be mindful. It's a beautiful, lifelong journey.

You are already better for just learning about it and approaching it with an open mind. We all make mistakes, but we can ask for forgiveness and repair what we can right away before it's too late.

Dealing with stress and worry

Nothing derails our life like unexpected events, stress, worry, anxiety, and troubles that pop out of nowhere. Our expectations are high, and our future plans are positive. We don't want stress and worry to overcome us, but so often it does. Such is life. The key is what happens when it plagues you. Where do you turn?

Fear is very real and is often behind most of our stress and worry. We have an inner monologue telling us we are not good enough. When we listen to the voice, fear of failure and disaster can become louder than any other positive message. Just like with anger, there are often emotions hidden underneath that we have to uncover. Fear is one emotion that lies at the center, and it is something we have to confront.

Just like exposure therapy, where a person afraid to speak in public may be given an opportunity to prepare a short speech in front of an audience, we may need to try exposure therapy for our fear. What if instead of running away from things because we are afraid, we made a plan and confronted them?

If you are suffering from anxiety while traveling on an airplane, it might be wise to lay out a plan for your next trip. If you are fearful during takeoff or landing, prepare a playlist on your phone to play for that time. If you worry about not having access to things or a bathroom or medicine, make sure you pack well and request a seat where you will feel most comfortable.

Mindfulness is being aware of your surroundings and of yourself. As much as we want others to take care of us, we know best what we need. Prepare yourself well and manage your expectations. If you act like nothing bothers you, you are not being realistic. Be honest and take care of yourself. What if your partner feared riding in a plane? What would you do to make that experience better for them? Now turn that around and get creative for yourself.

Breaking bad habits or negative behaviors

Can mindfulness help you quit negative or embarrassing habits? It's not a quick fix or an easy one, but because mindfulness helps your brain create new pathways for good habits, it's possible to make small improvements over time.

Before you get started, you have to be aware of exactly what the habit is and what changes you want to make. It gives you a chance to ask yourself why exactly you do what you do and how you feel about it.

You have to train your brain. Replace the bad habit with a new habit. For example, author Holly Whitaker decided to quit alcohol and made it a part of her morning routine to drink hot lemon water. She says in her book, Quit Like a Woman, "Today my toolbox consists of breathing techniques, hot lemon water, herbal tea, hot baths, cold showers (this is called "hydrotherapy" and it's so, so good), coffee, essential oils, yoga, meditation, kirtan, autonomous sensory meridian response (ASMR), massage, French pastries, emotional freedom technique (EFT), and many other things."

It's also helpful to pinpoint where your temptation occurs. Most of our everyday actions, good and bad and indifferent, happen at the same place every day. Think about where you brush your teeth, turn off your alarm, or talk with your coworkers. Familiarity can fool us, and that's where we need to acknowledge our temptations. Instead of reaching for that donut in the morning meeting, pack apple slices instead or research healthy alternatives that still taste great, like hazelnut spread or dark chocolate.

Whatever your habit is, create a toolbox to help you combat the cravings and fill the gap with something healthy and positive. You can use mindful walking, breathwork, or any other techniques we have talked about in this book. Get specific and get practical so that it is very clear to you what your priorities are.

Managing anger and hurt

Anger is a difficult emotion to deal with, as it brings out vulnerable sides to us that sometimes we would rather ignore. When you become angry, notice what it does to your body and pause before it controls you.

Anger can become rage quickly if you are not aware of what's going on. Has a boundary been crossed? Are you disappointed that your expectations are not being met? Do you feel ashamed, embarrassed, or "less than" in some way?

Anger and hurt coincide. They will not go away once you decide to incorporate mindfulness into your life and daily patterns. You will need to practice self-control by identifying your triggers, using your coping mechanisms, and breathing techniques to calm yourself down.

Mindfulness is a companion to you as you sort out all these thoughts and emotions.

Conclusion

What a journey this has been! You are no longer a total rookie when it comes to mindfulness. You are well on your way to a self-aware lifestyle that will bring so much peace and joy to you and others. Congratulations on learning about the basics, as well as specific techniques to help you compile your mindfulness toolbox.

Think back to what you thought mindfulness was at first. Did you equate it with meditation? Were you intimidated? Did you worry about whether or not it was going to "work for you"?

And now, here you are. You have taken a deep dive and learned more about yourself and the process of becoming more aware and present in every situation. This is an accomplishment! You should celebrate it, for it is no small thing. You made a choice to better yourself and the lives of those around you, and you should be proud and grateful.

We began with the basics of what mindfulness is and isn't and how the components of mindfulness set the stage for mindful living. You learned about having a beginner's mind and the difference between human being and human doing.

You are now armed with many techniques to practice mindfulness and pay attention to your breath. Your tool belt is locked and loaded with various methods to take with you as you explore mindfulness in your daily life. Don't forget the anchoring techniques when your mind wanders.

As you walk down this path of mindfulness, don't get discouraged when weeds and vines pop up and try to drag you down. Keep going. Don't give up. There are many more resources online and books that will help you further, you have what it takes within yourself. As Oliver Wendell Holmes said, "What lies before us and what lies behind us are tiny matters compared to what lies within us."

Thank you for making it through to the end of this book. Let's hope it was informative and able to provide you with all of the tools you need to achieve your goals.

Finally, if you found this book useful in any way, a review on Amazon is always appreciated!

Journal

DATE _/_/_

I WOKE UP FEELING

☐	CHEERFUL	☐	REFLECTIVE
☐	CALM	☐	ROMANTIC
☐	LIGHTHEARTED	☐	HOPEFUL
☐	GLOOMY	☐	TENSE
☐	STREESED	☐	BORED
☐	ANGRY	☐	CONFIDENT
☐	ANXIOUS	☐	MOTIVATED
☐	GRATEFUL	☐	OTHER

MY INTENTION FOR THE DAY

_____

_____

TODAYS CHALLENGES

_____

_____

_____

_____

MEDITATION:

TIME:	DESCRIBE YOUR EXPERIENCE
TYPE:	

RATE YOUR ABILITY TO REMAIN PRESENT TODAY

1   2   3   4   5   6   7   8   9   10

TODAYS MAJOR DISTRACTION

_____

_____

_____

_____

MY MOOD AT THE END OF THE DAY

_____

_____

_____

_____

FINAL THOUGHTS TO SEND ME TO SLEEP

_____

_____

_____

_____

DATE _/_/_

I WOKE UP FEELING

☐	CHEERFUL	☐	REFLECTIVE
☐	CALM	☐	ROMANTIC
☐	LIGHTHEARTED	☐	HOPEFUL
☐	GLOOMY	☐	TENSE
☐	STREESED	☐	BORED
☐	ANGRY	☐	CONFIDENT
☐	ANXIOUS	☐	MOTIVATED
☐	GRATEFUL	☐	OTHER

MY INTENTION FOR THE DAY

_____

_____

TODAYS CHALLENGES

_____

_____

_____

_____

MEDITATION:

TIME:	DESCRIBE YOUR EXPERIENCE
TYPE:	

RATE YOUR ABILITY TO REMAIN PRESENT TODAY

1   2   3   4   5   6   7   8   9   10

TODAYS MAJOR DISTRACTION

_____

_____

_____

_____

MY MOOD AT THE END OF THE DAY

_____

_____

_____

_____

FINAL THOUGHTS TO SEND ME TO SLEEP

_____

_____

_____

_____

DATE _/_/_

I WOKE UP FEELING

☐ CHEERFUL	☐ REFLECTIVE
☐ CALM	☐ ROMANTIC
☐ LIGHTHEARTED	☐ HOPEFUL
☐ GLOOMY	☐ TENSE
☐ STREESED	☐ BORED
☐ ANGRY	☐ CONFIDENT
☐ ANXIOUS	☐ MOTIVATED
☐ GRATEFUL	☐ OTHER

MY INTENTION FOR THE DAY

_____

_____

TODAYS CHALLENGES

_____

_____

_____

_____

MEDITATION:

TIME:	DESCRIBE YOUR EXPERIENCE
TYPE:	

RATE YOUR ABILITY TO REMAIN PRESENT TODAY

1   2   3   4   5   6   7   8   9   10

TODAYS MAJOR DISTRACTION

_____

_____

_____

_____

MY MOOD AT THE END OF THE DAY

_____

_____

_____

_____

FINAL THOUGHTS TO SEND ME TO SLEEP

_____

_____

_____

_____

DATE _/_/_

I WOKE UP FEELING

☐	CHEERFUL	☐	REFLECTIVE
☐	CALM	☐	ROMANTIC
☐	LIGHTHEARTED	☐	HOPEFUL
☐	GLOOMY	☐	TENSE
☐	STREESED	☐	BORED
☐	ANGRY	☐	CONFIDENT
☐	ANXIOUS	☐	MOTIVATED
☐	GRATEFUL	☐	OTHER

MY INTENTION FOR THE DAY

_____

_____

TODAYS CHALLENGES

_____

_____

_____

_____

MEDITATION:

TIME:	DESCRIBE YOUR EXPERIENCE
TYPE:	

RATE YOUR ABILITY TO REMAIN PRESENT TODAY

1   2   3   4   5   6   7   8   9   10

TODAYS MAJOR DISTRACTION

_____

_____

_____

_____

MY MOOD AT THE END OF THE DAY

_____

_____

_____

_____

FINAL THOUGHTS TO SEND ME TO SLEEP

_____

_____

_____

_____

DATE _/_/_

I WOKE UP FEELING

☐	CHEERFUL	☐	REFLECTIVE
☐	CALM	☐	ROMANTIC
☐	LIGHTHEARTED	☐	HOPEFUL
☐	GLOOMY	☐	TENSE
☐	STREESED	☐	BORED
☐	ANGRY	☐	CONFIDENT
☐	ANXIOUS	☐	MOTIVATED
☐	GRATEFUL	☐	OTHER

MY INTENTION FOR THE DAY

_____

_____

TODAYS CHALLENGES

_____

_____

_____

_____

MEDITATION:

TIME:	DESCRIBE YOUR EXPERIENCE
TYPE:	

RATE YOUR ABILITY TO REMAIN PRESENT TODAY

1   2   3   4   5   6   7   8   9   10

TODAYS MAJOR DISTRACTION

_____

_____

_____

_____

MY MOOD AT THE END OF THE DAY

_____

_____

_____

_____

FINAL THOUGHTS TO SEND ME TO SLEEP

_____

_____

_____

_____

DATE _/_/_

I WOKE UP FEELING

☐	CHEERFUL	☐	REFLECTIVE
☐	CALM	☐	ROMANTIC
☐	LIGHTHEARTED	☐	HOPEFUL
☐	GLOOMY	☐	TENSE
☐	STREESED	☐	BORED
☐	ANGRY	☐	CONFIDENT
☐	ANXIOUS	☐	MOTIVATED
☐	GRATEFUL	☐	OTHER

MY INTENTION FOR THE DAY

_____

_____

TODAYS CHALLENGES

_____

_____

_____

_____

MEDITATION:

TIME: TYPE:	DESCRIBE YOUR EXPERIENCE

RATE YOUR ABILITY TO REMAIN PRESENT TODAY

1   2   3   4   5   6   7   8   9   10

TODAYS MAJOR DISTRACTION

_____

_____

_____

_____

MY MOOD AT THE END OF THE DAY

_____

_____

_____

_____

FINAL THOUGHTS TO SEND ME TO SLEEP

_____

_____

_____

_____

DATE _/_/_

I WOKE UP FEELING

☐	CHEERFUL	☐	REFLECTIVE
☐	CALM	☐	ROMANTIC
☐	LIGHTHEARTED	☐	HOPEFUL
☐	GLOOMY	☐	TENSE
☐	STREESED	☐	BORED
☐	ANGRY	☐	CONFIDENT
☐	ANXIOUS	☐	MOTIVATED
☐	GRATEFUL	☐	OTHER

MY INTENTION FOR THE DAY

_____

_____

TODAYS CHALLENGES

_____

_____

_____

_____

MEDITATION:

TIME: TYPE:	DESCRIBE YOUR EXPERIENCE

RATE YOUR ABILITY TO REMAIN PRESENT TODAY

1   2   3   4   5   6   7   8   9   10

TODAYS MAJOR DISTRACTION

_____

_____

_____

_____

MY MOOD AT THE END OF THE DAY

_____

_____

_____

_____

FINAL THOUGHTS TO SEND ME TO SLEEP

_____

_____

_____

_____

_____

DATE _/_/_

I WOKE UP FEELING

☐ CHEERFUL	☐ REFLECTIVE
☐ CALM	☐ ROMANTIC
☐ LIGHTHEARTED	☐ HOPEFUL
☐ GLOOMY	☐ TENSE
☐ STREESED	☐ BORED
☐ ANGRY	☐ CONFIDENT
☐ ANXIOUS	☐ MOTIVATED
☐ GRATEFUL	☐ OTHER

MY INTENTION FOR THE DAY

_____

_____

TODAYS CHALLENGES

_____

_____

_____

_____

MEDITATION:

| TIME:

TYPE:	DESCRIBE YOUR EXPERIENCE

RATE YOUR ABILITY TO REMAIN PRESENT TODAY

1   2   3   4   5   6   7   8   9   10

TODAYS MAJOR DISTRACTION

_____

_____

_____

_____

MY MOOD AT THE END OF THE DAY

_____

_____

_____

_____

FINAL THOUGHTS TO SEND ME TO SLEEP

_____

_____

_____

_____

_____

DATE _/_/_

I WOKE UP FEELING

☐	CHEERFUL	☐	REFLECTIVE
☐	CALM	☐	ROMANTIC
☐	LIGHTHEARTED	☐	HOPEFUL
☐	GLOOMY	☐	TENSE
☐	STREESED	☐	BORED
☐	ANGRY	☐	CONFIDENT
☐	ANXIOUS	☐	MOTIVATED
☐	GRATEFUL	☐	OTHER

MY INTENTION FOR THE DAY

_____

_____

TODAYS CHALLENGES

_____

_____

_____

_____

MEDITATION:

TIME:	DESCRIBE YOUR EXPERIENCE
TYPE:	

RATE YOUR ABILITY TO REMAIN PRESENT TODAY

1   2   3   4   5   6   7   8   9   10

TODAYS MAJOR DISTRACTION

_____

_____

_____

_____

MY MOOD AT THE END OF THE DAY

_____

_____

_____

_____

FINAL THOUGHTS TO SEND ME TO SLEEP

_____

_____

_____

_____

DATE _/_/_

I WOKE UP FEELING

☐ CHEERFUL	☐ REFLECTIVE
☐ CALM	☐ ROMANTIC
☐ LIGHTHEARTED	☐ HOPEFUL
☐ GLOOMY	☐ TENSE
☐ STREESED	☐ BORED
☐ ANGRY	☐ CONFIDENT
☐ ANXIOUS	☐ MOTIVATED
☐ GRATEFUL	☐ OTHER

MY INTENTION FOR THE DAY

_____

_____

TODAYS CHALLENGES

_____

_____

_____

_____

MEDITATION:

TIME:	DESCRIBE YOUR EXPERIENCE
TYPE:	

118

RATE YOUR ABILITY TO REMAIN PRESENT TODAY

1   2   3   4   5   6   7   8   9   10

TODAYS MAJOR DISTRACTION

_____

_____

_____

_____

MY MOOD AT THE END OF THE DAY

_____

_____

_____

_____

FINAL THOUGHTS TO SEND ME TO SLEEP

_____

_____

_____

_____

DATE _/_/_

I WOKE UP FEELING

☐	CHEERFUL	☐	REFLECTIVE
☐	CALM	☐	ROMANTIC
☐	LIGHTHEARTED	☐	HOPEFUL
☐	GLOOMY	☐	TENSE
☐	STREESED	☐	BORED
☐	ANGRY	☐	CONFIDENT
☐	ANXIOUS	☐	MOTIVATED
☐	GRATEFUL	☐	OTHER

MY INTENTION FOR THE DAY

_____

_____

TODAYS CHALLENGES

_____

_____

_____

_____

MEDITATION:

TIME:	DESCRIBE YOUR EXPERIENCE
TYPE:	

RATE YOUR ABILITY TO REMAIN PRESENT TODAY

1   2   3   4   5   6   7   8   9   10

TODAYS MAJOR DISTRACTION

_____

_____

_____

_____

MY MOOD AT THE END OF THE DAY

_____

_____

_____

_____

FINAL THOUGHTS TO SEND ME TO SLEEP

_____

_____

_____

_____

_____

DATE _/_/_

I WOKE UP FEELING

☐	CHEERFUL	☐	REFLECTIVE
☐	CALM	☐	ROMANTIC
☐	LIGHTHEARTED	☐	HOPEFUL
☐	GLOOMY	☐	TENSE
☐	STREESED	☐	BORED
☐	ANGRY	☐	CONFIDENT
☐	ANXIOUS	☐	MOTIVATED
☐	GRATEFUL	☐	OTHER

MY INTENTION FOR THE DAY

_____

_____

TODAYS CHALLENGES

_____

_____

_____

_____

MEDITATION:

TIME:	DESCRIBE YOUR EXPERIENCE
TYPE:	

RATE YOUR ABILITY TO REMAIN PRESENT TODAY

1   2   3   4   5   6   7   8   9   10

TODAYS MAJOR DISTRACTION

_____

_____

_____

_____

MY MOOD AT THE END OF THE DAY

_____

_____

_____

_____

FINAL THOUGHTS TO SEND ME TO SLEEP

_____

_____

_____

_____

_____

DATE _/_/_

I WOKE UP FEELING

☐	CHEERFUL	☐	REFLECTIVE
☐	CALM	☐	ROMANTIC
☐	LIGHTHEARTED	☐	HOPEFUL
☐	GLOOMY	☐	TENSE
☐	STREESED	☐	BORED
☐	ANGRY	☐	CONFIDENT
☐	ANXIOUS	☐	MOTIVATED
☐	GRATEFUL	☐	OTHER

MY INTENTION FOR THE DAY

_____

_____

TODAYS CHALLENGES

_____

_____

_____

_____

MEDITATION:

TIME:	DESCRIBE YOUR EXPERIENCE
TYPE:	

RATE YOUR ABILITY TO REMAIN PRESENT TODAY

1   2   3   4   5   6   7   8   9   10

TODAYS MAJOR DISTRACTION

_____

_____

_____

_____

MY MOOD AT THE END OF THE DAY

_____

_____

_____

_____

FINAL THOUGHTS TO SEND ME TO SLEEP

_____

_____

_____

_____

DATE _/_/_

I WOKE UP FEELING

☐	CHEERFUL	☐	REFLECTIVE
☐	CALM	☐	ROMANTIC
☐	LIGHTHEARTED	☐	HOPEFUL
☐	GLOOMY	☐	TENSE
☐	STREESED	☐	BORED
☐	ANGRY	☐	CONFIDENT
☐	ANXIOUS	☐	MOTIVATED
☐	GRATEFUL	☐	OTHER

MY INTENTION FOR THE DAY

_____

_____

TODAYS CHALLENGES

_____

_____

_____

_____

MEDITATION:

| TIME:

TYPE:	DESCRIBE YOUR EXPERIENCE

RATE YOUR ABILITY TO REMAIN PRESENT TODAY

1   2   3   4   5   6   7   8   9   10

TODAYS MAJOR DISTRACTION

_____

_____

_____

_____

MY MOOD AT THE END OF THE DAY

_____

_____

_____

_____

FINAL THOUGHTS TO SEND ME TO SLEEP

_____

_____

_____

_____

DATE _/_/_

I WOKE UP FEELING

☐	CHEERFUL	☐	REFLECTIVE
☐	CALM	☐	ROMANTIC
☐	LIGHTHEARTED	☐	HOPEFUL
☐	GLOOMY	☐	TENSE
☐	STREESED	☐	BORED
☐	ANGRY	☐	CONFIDENT
☐	ANXIOUS	☐	MOTIVATED
☐	GRATEFUL	☐	OTHER

MY INTENTION FOR THE DAY

_____

_____

TODAYS CHALLENGES

_____

_____

_____

_____

MEDITATION:

TIME: TYPE:	DESCRIBE YOUR EXPERIENCE

RATE YOUR ABILITY TO REMAIN PRESENT TODAY

1   2   3   4   5   6   7   8   9   10

TODAYS MAJOR DISTRACTION

_____

_____

_____

_____

MY MOOD AT THE END OF THE DAY

_____

_____

_____

_____

FINAL THOUGHTS TO SEND ME TO SLEEP

_____

_____

_____

_____

_____

DATE _/_/_

I WOKE UP FEELING

☐	CHEERFUL	☐ REFLECTIVE
☐	CALM	☐ ROMANTIC
☐	LIGHTHEARTED	☐ HOPEFUL
☐	GLOOMY	☐ TENSE
☐	STREESED	☐ BORED
☐	ANGRY	☐ CONFIDENT
☐	ANXIOUS	☐ MOTIVATED
☐	GRATEFUL	☐ OTHER

MY INTENTION FOR THE DAY

_____

_____

TODAYS CHALLENGES

_____

_____

_____

_____

MEDITATION:

TIME:	DESCRIBE YOUR EXPERIENCE
TYPE:	

RATE YOUR ABILITY TO REMAIN PRESENT TODAY

1   2   3   4   5   6   7   8   9   10

TODAYS MAJOR DISTRACTION

_____

_____

_____

_____

MY MOOD AT THE END OF THE DAY

_____

_____

_____

_____

FINAL THOUGHTS TO SEND ME TO SLEEP

_____

_____

_____

_____

DATE _/_/_

I WOKE UP FEELING

☐	CHEERFUL	☐	REFLECTIVE
☐	CALM	☐	ROMANTIC
☐	LIGHTHEARTED	☐	HOPEFUL
☐	GLOOMY	☐	TENSE
☐	STREESED	☐	BORED
☐	ANGRY	☐	CONFIDENT
☐	ANXIOUS	☐	MOTIVATED
☐	GRATEFUL	☐	OTHER

MY INTENTION FOR THE DAY

_____

_____

TODAYS CHALLENGES

_____

_____

_____

_____

MEDITATION:

TIME:	DESCRIBE YOUR EXPERIENCE
TYPE:	

RATE YOUR ABILITY TO REMAIN PRESENT TODAY

1   2   3   4   5   6   7   8   9   10

TODAYS MAJOR DISTRACTION

_____

_____

_____

_____

MY MOOD AT THE END OF THE DAY

_____

_____

_____

_____

FINAL THOUGHTS TO SEND ME TO SLEEP

_____

_____

_____

_____

_____

DATE _/_/_

I WOKE UP FEELING

☐	CHEERFUL	☐	REFLECTIVE
☐	CALM	☐	ROMANTIC
☐	LIGHTHEARTED	☐	HOPEFUL
☐	GLOOMY	☐	TENSE
☐	STREESED	☐	BORED
☐	ANGRY	☐	CONFIDENT
☐	ANXIOUS	☐	MOTIVATED
☐	GRATEFUL	☐	OTHER

MY INTENTION FOR THE DAY

_____

_____

TODAYS CHALLENGES

_____

_____

_____

_____

MEDITATION:

TIME:	DESCRIBE YOUR EXPERIENCE
TYPE:	

RATE YOUR ABILITY TO REMAIN PRESENT TODAY

1   2   3   4   5   6   7   8   9   10

TODAYS MAJOR DISTRACTION

_____

_____

_____

_____

MY MOOD AT THE END OF THE DAY

_____

_____

_____

_____

FINAL THOUGHTS TO SEND ME TO SLEEP

_____

_____

_____

_____

DATE _/_/_

I WOKE UP FEELING

☐	CHEERFUL	☐	REFLECTIVE
☐	CALM	☐	ROMANTIC
☐	LIGHTHEARTED	☐	HOPEFUL
☐	GLOOMY	☐	TENSE
☐	STREESED	☐	BORED
☐	ANGRY	☐	CONFIDENT
☐	ANXIOUS	☐	MOTIVATED
☐	GRATEFUL	☐	OTHER

MY INTENTION FOR THE DAY

_____

_____

TODAYS CHALLENGES

_____

_____

_____

_____

MEDITATION:

TIME:	DESCRIBE YOUR EXPERIENCE
TYPE:	

RATE YOUR ABILITY TO REMAIN PRESENT TODAY

1   2   3   4   5   6   7   8   9   10

TODAYS MAJOR DISTRACTION

_____

_____

_____

_____

MY MOOD AT THE END OF THE DAY

_____

_____

_____

_____

FINAL THOUGHTS TO SEND ME TO SLEEP

_____

_____

_____

_____

_____

DATE _/_/_

I WOKE UP FEELING

☐ CHEERFUL	☐ REFLECTIVE
☐ CALM	☐ ROMANTIC
☐ LIGHTHEARTED	☐ HOPEFUL
☐ GLOOMY	☐ TENSE
☐ STREESED	☐ BORED
☐ ANGRY	☐ CONFIDENT
☐ ANXIOUS	☐ MOTIVATED
☐ GRATEFUL	☐ OTHER

MY INTENTION FOR THE DAY

_____

_____

TODAYS CHALLENGES

_____

_____

_____

_____

MEDITATION:

TIME:	DESCRIBE YOUR EXPERIENCE
TYPE:	

RATE YOUR ABILITY TO REMAIN PRESENT TODAY

1   2   3   4   5   6   7   8   9   10

TODAYS MAJOR DISTRACTION

_____

_____

_____

_____

MY MOOD AT THE END OF THE DAY

_____

_____

_____

_____

FINAL THOUGHTS TO SEND ME TO SLEEP

_____

_____

_____

_____

DATE _/_/_

I WOKE UP FEELING

☐ CHEERFUL		☐ REFLECTIVE	
☐ CALM		☐ ROMANTIC	
☐ LIGHTHEARTED		☐ HOPEFUL	
☐ GLOOMY		☐ TENSE	
☐ STREESED		☐ BORED	
☐ ANGRY		☐ CONFIDENT	
☐ ANXIOUS		☐ MOTIVATED	
☐ GRATEFUL		☐ OTHER	

MY INTENTION FOR THE DAY

_____

_____

TODAYS CHALLENGES

_____

_____

_____

_____

MEDITATION:

| TIME:

TYPE:	DESCRIBE YOUR EXPERIENCE

RATE YOUR ABILITY TO REMAIN PRESENT TODAY

1   2   3   · 4   5   6   7   8   9   10

TODAYS MAJOR DISTRACTION

_____

_____

_____

_____

MY MOOD AT THE END OF THE DAY

_____

_____

_____

_____

FINAL THOUGHTS TO SEND ME TO SLEEP

_____

_____

_____

_____

_____

About Author

Natalie Morgon is a mental health counselor, poet, author, and speaker devoted to empowering people to love themselves and transform their lives. Natalie Morgon has more than 15 years of counseling experience. Natalie has become the woman she is today, overcoming the death of a loved one, domestic violence, eating disorders, and divorce. Natalie is passionate about the power of the right mindset to change the course of a person's life, and she channels this passion into her writing. Her work explores strategies for changing your mindset to pave the way for success in any field.

Printed in Great Britain
by Amazon

29900926R00081